ANNIHILATION FROM WITHIN

FRED CHARLES IKLÉ

ANNIHILATION FROM WITHIN

THE ULTIMATE THREAT TO NATIONS

Columbia University Press

New York

Columbia University Press
Publishers Since 1893
New York   Chichester, West Sussex

Copyright © 2006 Fred Charles Iklé
All rights reserved

Library of Congress Cataloging-in-Publication Data
Iklé, Fred Charles.
Annihilation from within :
the ultimate threat to nations / Fred Charles Iklé.
p.   cm.
Includes bibliographical references and index.
ISBN 0-231-13952-7 (cloth : alk. paper)
1. Security, International.   2. Technology—Social aspects.
3. Terrorism.   4. Radicalism.   5. Nuclear disarmament.
I. Title.   JZ5595.I35 2006
355'.033—dc22   2006019331

Columbia University Press books are printed on
permanent and durable acid-free paper.

Printed in the United States of America

c 10 9 8 7 6 5 4 3 2 1

CONTENTS

WHAT THIS BOOK IS ABOUT

THE STORY LINE OF THIS BOOK IS AT ONCE FORWARD-LOOKING AND HISTORICAL. The prospect ahead features revolutionary new threats to national security and could end in demolition of the existing world order. Looking backward, the story traces this coming upheaval to historic forces that have been centuries in the making. Today's menaces—jihadist terrorism, rogue nations producing nuclear bombs—may be viewed as mere symptoms of these forces, as the rustling wind that foretells the gathering storm. Few military strategists and political experts have grasped the dimensions of the storm awaiting us. Fewer still are mindful of its historic evolution.

The emerging crisis is the outgrowth of technological progress. It reflects the dark side of progress. Globalization guarantees the ceaseless spread of new technologies, whether beneficial or destructive. The nuclear age offers the clearest lesson of this problem. Until the end of the Cold War, it appeared that we were somehow managing the nuclear threat. Over a span of half a century, the political and military leaders of the nuclear powers were able to pursue strategies that averted the use of nuclear weapons. Their long-run success in maintaining the regime of "non-use" is one of the greatest achievements in the history of military strategy.

Alas, the world is now different. After our stressful journey through the Cold War—a journey with a happy ending—we now face a ghastly new predicament. One nation after another is starting up nuclear programs, allegedly for peaceful purposes, but often and obviously as a stratagem for getting to an arsenal of nuclear weapons. And the proliferation problem does not end there. A cascade of frightening news reports tells us that the control of national governments over nuclear materials and bombs is far from secure. The inescapable subtext of these reports is that, all too soon, we must expect these weapons to be acquired by doomsday cults, anarchists, and terrorist gangs.

Other technologies, not yet on the radar screens of the world's media, will be even more resistant to political control. It is well known that immensely beneficial advances in the life sciences can be misused to develop biological weapons. But the most revolutionary impact of the life sciences might be the most difficult to control: the conquest of the human mind by brain science. A vast enhancement in intelligent decision-making might be just decades away. Some powerful nations have already built elaborate command and decision centers that exploit the capabilities of the latest computer systems. As day follows night, these projects will gradually take advantage of the rapid advances in brain science to complement the strengths of computers with the unique capabilities of the human brain. If these projects are successful, they will achieve a superhuman intelligence able to trump the performance of first-rate human experts and the latest super-computers. Any such leap forward in intelligent decision-making would be a change comparable to the evolution from primates to *Homo sapiens*. The transition would pose the most fundamental challenge to all religions. It would upend human civilization. It would instantly obliterate all previous notions about relative national power. And in light of our experience with nuclear proliferation, it would be absurd to expect the United Nations to "control" this new intelligence. Today, the United States uses computerized command centers for its military leaders, while China is experimenting with computerized decision centers that can serve both the military and its political leadership. If China moved ahead of America in the race to develop superhuman intelligence systems, would the U.S. Government wait for UN approval to catch up?

Today, our policymakers and analysts are preoccupied with terrorist attacks by militant Islamists. These attacks, often by suicide bombers, have been painful and enormously costly for the victims, but they cannot defeat established democracies or indeed any nation that is not already a failed state. The fact is that contemporary Islamic terrorism does not have a strategy for victory. It is swayed by impulses animated by a fervidness for revenge and religious utopias. It is as if these jihadist terrorists—enraged by their impotence—seek gratification from bloodshed and self-immolation. While these murderous assaults hurt us, they also spur us to increase our military power and to strengthen the defense of our homeland. What does not kill us makes us stronger.

Yet terrorists, anarchists, and other evildoers seek to acquire weapons of mass destruction, and some of them are bound to succeed. Most of them will merely want to use these weapons to inflict immense damage without knowing how to achieve a lasting victory. But keep in mind that, throughout history, mankind had to suffer the depredations of leaders who can rally throngs of followers and intimidate the masses. The twentieth century offers vivid examples. Among such historic evildoers, the most relevant in this context are Lenin and Hitler. The greatest threat to the world order in this century will be the next Hitler or Lenin, a charismatic leader who combines utter ruthlessness with a brilliant strategic sense, cunning, and boundless ambition—and who gains control over just a few weapons of mass destruction.

This new threat, still offstage, now awaits us. Any such evil but charismatic leader will be able to attack a major nation from within even if that nation possesses enormous military strength and capable police forces. If this new tyrant turns out to be strategically intelligent, he could prepare to launch a couple of mass destruction weapons against carefully chosen targets—without training camps in another nation, without help from a foreign terrorist organization, without a military campaign across the nation's borders. He would thus offer no targets for retaliation and render useless a nation's most powerful deterrent forces. By contrast, an expanding caliphate—the utopia that jihadists dream about—would offer the leading democracies plenty of easy targets for retaliation.

The purpose of this new tyrant would not be to destroy landmark buildings, highjack airplanes, attack railroad stations and religious shrines. His aim would be to paralyze the national leadership and spread nationwide panic, to ensure that the center could not hold. He would be well prepared to exploit this chaos by seizing complete control of the nation's government and imposing his dictatorship. Success in any such endeavor would be a shattering event, signifying to democracies everywhere that their world, their basic institutions, their national security strategies, their citizens' everyday lives—that all this was now up for grabs. Living comfortably on borrowed time, most democratic societies lack the will and foresight needed to defend against any such calamity.

Non-democratic governments will also be vulnerable—indeed, more vulnerable—to annihilation from within. In those Central Asian republics, for example, where authoritarian rulers confront large Muslim populations who want a fundamentalist Islamic state, the detonation of a single nuclear bomb in the capital would create a political vacuum. This could enable a religious leader (perhaps a cleric like Iraq's Muqtada al-Sadr) to mobilize his throngs of followers and seize control of the country.

Today's military planners have not given much thought to averting annihilation from within. The conventional wisdom about the world's future holds that it is steadily becoming more democratic and therefore more peaceful. Technological progress is said to make all countries interdependent—to push us toward a unified world in which distance is no longer an impediment to travel and trade and, thanks to the Internet, has been erased entirely as an obstacle to communications. The appealing vision of a new "flat world" has left many commentators blind to the dark side of technological progress.

THE HISTORICAL PASSAGES IN THIS BOOK explain the origins of our new predicament. If we hope to navigate our way past the deadly threats confronting us, it will help to understand the roots and evolution of the historic forces that have unleashed them. They originated some 250 years ago in Western Europe, in a schism in mankind's culture. Science was rather suddenly freed from political and religious controls. The ascendance of Enlightenment thinking diminished the influence of religious beliefs, a development in which the Protestant Reformation also played a role. And government policies that increasingly promoted a free market served to promote, and handsomely reward, technological advances.

Since then, technological progress has brought immense improvements in the human condition. These gains seemed to outweigh all the potential applications of technology that would be destructive or harmful. But surprisingly, already at the very beginning of the Industrial Revolution, many thinkers had a foreboding of technology's dark side. And today we begin to understand the dangerous dynamic of the cultural schism.

As a result of this schism, two modes of human thought and activity split apart. One mode is animated by religious faiths, ethnic and national traditions, and societal customs. This mode remained essentially the same as it had been before the schism. It shapes the basic structure of society and nourishes the sense of patriotism and loyalty that enables nations to function. But the other mode of thinking is guided by science, which seeks to understand the workings of nature by relying on empirical verification, not on a definition of "truth" handed down through generations. Our growing knowledge of the physical universe has enabled us to transform our environment progressively and to alter the human condition. Following the initial cultural schism, the accelerating scientific and technological progress gave us the Industrial Revolution, which in turn spread progress to more and more countries and changed the face of our planet.

One might plausibly observe that this story is old hat. But what the standard narrative leaves out is the most important part of the saga, namely that the cultural schism is *still* widening—and dangerously so. Technological progress and the global political order march to different drummers.

Science makes cumulative discoveries and hence can advance at an accelerating pace. It has acquired an inner dynamic of progress that is nearly self-sustaining. But the sphere of government and international affairs is marked by alternating periods of advance and decline, of gains and losses. Individual liberty expands and is suppressed again. Peace is followed by war and war by a new peace. Religious tolerance is followed by theocratic repression, to be replaced by a more secular regime. Periods of free trade are followed by protectionism and again by new efforts to spread free trade. In sum, the political, social, and religious sphere moves in a zigzag course, while science makes cumulative advances.

The two modes of human thought and activity that split apart some 250 years ago are destined to drift farther apart because disparate aspirations of the two modes aggravate the widening schism. Science and technology do not have a final goal. They pursue a continuing conquest of nature in which disproved theories are replaced by new knowledge. But political endeavors have finite goals. Marxism did not aspire to be followed by capitalism, Islam does not seek to be replaced by Christianity,

America's propagation of democracy does not strive to be succeeded by autocratic governments.

This widening divergence in human culture might overwhelm the political order of the world in a way that endangers the survival of all nations. And, bear in mind, only sovereign nations can marshal troops and rally political support to defeat terrorist organizations, deter aggression, enforce UN decisions. When push comes to shove, only nations can keep some order in the world.

Annihilation from within is not a temporary peril, but the end point and ultimate impact of this elemental historic force that has gained ever more strength over two centuries. Military history offers no lessons that tell nations how to cope with a continuing global dispersion of cataclysmic means for destruction. Because of the cultural split some 250 years ago, the threat of annihilation from within is now woven into the fabric of our era.

Let us admit it: mankind became entrapped in a Faustian bargain. In the famous medieval legend, Faust sells his soul to the devil in exchange for the magical powers of science (or rather the imagined powers of alchemy in those days). There is much that we can do to avert the worst disaster. But as we begin to discern the trials that lie ahead, our exuberance about unending progress is tempered by a premonition that our "bargain with the devil" might end badly.

ANNIHILATION FROM WITHIN

1

MANKIND'S CULTURAL SPLIT

Two souls, alas, dwell in my breast,
the one strives to forsake the other.
—GOETHE

WE LIVE AT A TIME OF OMINOUS CONTRADICTIONS. Our age is unceasingly revolutionary; yet the human race remains moored to ancient traditions. Technological advances bring us ever more wealth and longer lives; yet they also enable evildoers to inflict cataclysmic destruction. Weapons of mass destruction are feared by all nations; yet the scientific knowledge and wherewithal to make such weapons keeps proliferating across our planet. Every country counts on economic growth and wants to benefit from technological progress, yet this common interest neither blunts the clash of religions nor alleviates enmities between nations. Every one of these fateful contradictions is manmade, yet we do not know how to overcome them. We begin to apprehend with horror that we are trapped in our Faustian bargain.

To learn how to cope with this conflicted age, we first need to understand the historic forces that brought it about. Some 250 years ago, science began to pull apart from the other domains of human activity. This split in human culture allowed science and technology to move ahead at an accelerating pace.

It thus unleashed a relentless dynamic that transformed the face of the earth. It bestowed unprecedented wealth and military strength upon many nations. And it brought us to a pass in which two essentially incompatible modes of thinking now dominate our lives.

One mode is imbued with religious beliefs, ethnic customs, social and political values, and communal or national traditions. This mode remained the way it had been since the beginning of human civilization. As in the past, it still shapes the basic structure of human society. It provides the sense of obedience, power, and pride that makes governments function. It is the wellspring of common loyalty and shared memories that motivate religious movements, tribes, and nations—in war and peace. Political convictions that are anchored only in the intellect are blown away by the first ill wind, but convictions that are rooted in ancestral memories will survive adversity.

In the other mode of thinking, people became guided by scientific concepts and theories, and the truth is sought via empirical verification rather than tradition and faith. This kind of thinking and action has enabled mankind to transform its natural environment and to achieve enormous material gains. It is the reason why our world has changed more profoundly and more rapidly during the last two centuries than any time in the past. It explains why the population living on our planet has grown more than eightfold, why the world's economic production has increased 40-fold, why the life expectancy of young adults has doubled, and why distance as an impediment to travel, trade, and communication has been greatly reduced.

While this global transformation wrought by science and technology has drastically changed many aspects of the human condition, it left others nearly untouched. During the last two centuries, the basic architecture and building blocks of the political order of the world remained largely the same. The nation-state is the dominant political force in the world today, just as it was two hundred years ago. For all the chatter about globalization,

despite all the ebullient visions of mankind's universal inter-
dependence, no alternative has emerged to replace this familiar old structure. The United Nations, the World Bank, and so
far even the European Union are no substitutes. Without the
support of national governments, these organizations lack the
political power and physical resources to collect taxes for major
economic projects or to provide economic aid, let alone to carry
out a military campaign. To this day, only sovereign nations can
defeat a well-armed terrorist organization or marshal the military forces for "United Nations" peacekeeping. Only nations
can maintain the ideals and achievements of democracy.

And so the planet's land masses remain partitioned into national territories. This mosaic reflects many layers of history:
peace treaties signed long ago, conquests by cavalry forces and
sailing ships, the jigsaw maps that the colonial powers imposed
on Africa and the Middle East. The floor plan for the contemporary world order is like a palimpsest of old deeds and misdeeds
whose lines have been erased and redrawn many times. Yet its
organizing concept—separate territorial sovereignties—has
survived all the scientific, technological, and demographic revo-
lutions of the past two centuries.

How much longer can the political foundations of the international order remain largely unchanged while science and
technology keep transforming the world? So far, we do not feel
the full impact of mankind's cultural split. But we anxiously
watch harbingers of things to come: the resurgent spread of
mass destruction weapons, rumored dangers of nanotechnology, worried speculations about altering the human species.
The accelerating momentum of scientific discoveries and technological advances has become like a resistant infectious agent
that contaminated the human race some time ago. Today, we
still live in the quiescent incubation period. But beware! The
full virulence of this "infection" might not be far away.

To be sure, national governments, international organizations, and legions of ethicists will try to rein in the deleterious

effects of technology. On the evidence thus far, their efforts—whether in the form of legal regulations, arms control treaties, or appeals to moral restraint—have largely failed. The accelerating dynamic of science and technology is so perilous because the cultural split has separated it from effective political control.

This unprecedented human predicament is the theme that overarches my book.

A World of Two Souls

Even though the predicament is unprecedented, it was anticipated. Before the Industrial Revolution had reached its full strength, poets, writers, and artists had premonitions about the new historic force and the unfathomable changes it might bring. There is much in the Romanticist art of the late eighteenth and early nineteenth centuries—the music, paintings, and fiction—that speaks to the calm before the storm and reflects the tension between evanescent enjoyment and anxious anticipation. Examples are Beethoven's *Pastoral* Symphony, Caspar David Friedrich's paintings, Schubert's songs, John Keats's "Ode to a Nightingale," the paintings of still-pristine American landscapes by Albert Bierstadt or Thomas Cole, and of course many passages in Goethe's *Faust*.

Some writers used metaphorical stories to express their dark foreboding. In 1797, Goethe wrote *The Sorcerer's Apprentice*, a ballad about the irresponsible unleashing of a robot whose unstoppable energy spreads havoc all around. Two centuries later, *The Sorcerer's Apprentice* resonates with our concerns about the proliferation of nuclear technology. In 1816 Mary Shelley wrote the novel *Frankenstein or the Modern Prometheus* (published 1818), which became a highly popular book that spoke to the then-emerging fear that scientists might create humanlike beings who could inflict monstrous harm on society. To this day, the fear of future Frankensteins lives on in people's imagination—a fascinating story told well by Jon Turney.[1]

It is as if mankind now has two souls—"the one strives to forsake the other." One soul guided human development for millennia, inspiring people with religious faith, social sentiments, and cultural traditions. It embraces religions thousands of years old and political principles that had gained acceptance several hundred years ago. The other soul seeks scientific knowledge to expand the human conquest of nature. It reaches out to a horizon that is forever receding. During the past two hundred years, this second soul has inspired mankind to gain unprecedented power over natural forces. These advances, however, have not been matched in the political, social, and religious sphere. Our culture has become deeply divided.

Once we have come to understand this cultural split of the modern age, we need not look far to see examples. Consider, for instance, the American duality: the disjunction between the political foundations of the United States and its global role since World War II. What has endowed America's military and economic power with a global reach beyond that of any other nation is the vigorous development and exploitation of new technologies. What gives the United States its internal strength, pride, and cohesion, all essential for political and military influence abroad, are its Constitution and political traditions. The constitutional provisions critical for the values and functioning of the American republic are more than two hundred years old, save for a few vital amendments (above all, the amendments to abolish slavery and, also, the amendment on female suffrage). It seems fair to say that the essence of America's *political* order—its political soul—was created by a nation of fewer than four million inhabitants, more than two-thirds of whom worked on farms. After two hundred years, this "soul" still serves the nation splendidly, despite a 75-fold increase in the number of inhabitants, a huge expansion of the national territory, a vast transformation of the economy, and many other far-reaching changes. How long can America's two cultural spheres harmoniously sustain each other?

Before the cultural split, all civilizations had been unitary. Religious faiths, societal traditions, political thought, artistic and scientific endeavors, all were intimately connected and dominated the entire culture. This cultural dominion left little freedom for revolutionary technological advances. The exceptions—such as the exploitation of scientific discoveries to design navigation instruments, develop metallurgy, and improve calendars and clocks—are well remembered because they were so rare. Only a few scientists of extraordinary courage and intellectual strength ventured beyond the accepted norms of interpreting nature.

Until the eighteenth century, religious and political beliefs, and the ways of thinking about nature fostered by these beliefs, determined the flow of history. The belief systems ruled over the evolution of all civilizations and illuminated the horizon of human creativity. They forced the early manifestations of man's scientific and technological prowess to move in harmony with religion and the political order. They kept science in step with the evolution of society, instead of allowing it to race ahead. Being so closely intertwined, the two sides of human creativity shared their periods of flowering, times of stagnation, and periods of decline.

This harmony is marvelously illuminated by the fate of science and technology in China. Despite China's many astonishing scientific discoveries during and before Europe's Dark Age, it was to be more than a century after the scientific-technological revolution had swept through Europe, America, and Japan that Chinese science became emancipated from the constraining cultural sphere, and then only because of the impact of the West. In the early fifteenth century, China had acquired the knowledge and technical capabilities to navigate distant oceans. It could have become a major naval power. But in 1433 an edict by the Emperor Zhu Di put an abrupt end to any such adventures. Several scholars have sought to explain why the modern scientific-industrial age reached China so late—well after it had impacted Japan and Russia—when many scientific discoveries and masterful technical applications had blossomed in China so early. Wen-yuan Qian of the University of California in Los Angeles points to the "ideology of hierarchism" by which China "was shackled" for two hundred years, a way of conceptualizing the world that "explicitly endorses an obedient attitude, a self-contented outlook, and a pacifist stand to deal with an allegedly changeless world." Donald J. Munro of the University of Michigan's Center for Chinese Studies argues that even in the twentieth century, there remained traces of "old philosophical ideas about knowledge and inquiry . . . ideas rooted in neo-Confucian doctrines." In Munro's words, what diverted attention from the pursuit of scientific inquiry were "ideas about a totalistic world and about the style of inquiry derived from it." It seems that China's commitment to a "totalistic world" delayed the cultural split.[2]

So it happened that Western Europe was the first region of the world in which the pursuit of science began to diverge from religious beliefs and societal norms. This emancipation began stealthily, but in the seventeenth century it was increasingly accepted. Before that time, several of the intellectual pioneers—Giordano Bruno, Galileo Galilei—notoriously suffered death or imprisonment for their rebellion against the cultural unity that allowed religious teachings to circumscribe humanity's spiritual existence. The guardians of the religious and political order in the sixteenth and early seventeenth centuries resisted the initial efforts of scientists to break away from the unitary culture.

Although it is now standard practice to deride this suppression of scientific discovery, the European authorities of the late Middle Ages and the Renaissance surely deserve some credit for understanding what was at stake. They intuitively foresaw that a cultural schism would have revolutionary and dangerous consequences. Yet their unsuccessful and at times oppressive attempt to avert the schism now has few defenders. Even the Roman Catholic Church has felt obliged to express second thoughts, 350 years after it had sought to keep Galileo from opening one of the many fissures that eventually led to a world of two souls. In 1992, Pope John Paul II endorsed the findings of a lengthy investigation by the Pontifical Academy of Science that concluded Galileo Galilei had been wronged.

An extraordinary confluence of religious and political upheavals in Western Europe forced the early hairline fissures in European culture wide open and liberated science from political control. Prominent among these developments was the philosophy of the Enlightenment, which diminished the influence of religious belief on people's lives and thinking, and which in part was a delayed consequence of the Protestant Reformation. Additional blows to the unitary culture were delivered by new government policies, especially in Western Europe and the United States, that allowed the free market to promote and reward technological innovation.

Long before mankind's cultural divergence had reached its full scope and conquered the whole world, political philosophers and historians began to recognize its profoundly revolutionary character. Early in the nineteenth century, its most visible manifestations first emerged in England and became known as the Industrial Revolution—a term that John Stuart Mill had used already in 1848 and that became popularized in 1888 through lectures by the English economist Arnold Toynbee (the uncle of the historian Arnold J. Toynbee). There is wide agreement among historians that, in addition to scientific discoveries, the necessary precursors of the Industrial Revolution included changing attitudes toward religion, new ideas in political philosophy, and innovations in governmental practices and law.[3]

Although the scientific-industrial upheaval began in Western Europe, science and technology are not something intrinsically "Western." One might classify the Bill of Rights, classical music, and Protestantism as cultural contributions that are specifically Western. And one might note that from the seventeenth century onward, West European scholars were disproportionately represented among the titans of science. But empirical science is no more "Western" than mathematics is "Arab" because of the geographic provenance of algebra and Arabic numerals.[4] The fact is that any nation, regardless of how "non-Western" it is, can now carry out projects employing advanced scientific theories and technology if it has a sufficiently large educated class and the political will to marshal the requisite human and economic resources.

The cultural split is not linked to geographic location. All societies, wherever located, have by now experienced this split to varying degrees, as the scientific-technological mode of human thought has spread to all civilizations. The influential French historian Fernand Braudel—based on his useful distinction between "culture" and "civilization"—explained that "civilizations, vast or otherwise, can always be located on the map. An essential part of their character depends on the constraints or advantages of their geographical situation." [5] But in the cultural realm, such geographic constraints are no longer relevant to the scientific and technological mode of human activity. Since so many technological advances brought all civilizations immense economic benefits and vast improvements in health care, few people are concerned about the widening divergence between mankind's political culture and its scientific achievements. Zbigniew Brzezinski foresaw the political problems of this divergence thirty-five years ago: "On the one hand this [technological] revolution marks the beginning of a global community; on the other hand, it fragments humanity and detaches it from its traditional moorings." Somewhat similar ideas were expressed by Jacques Ellul (who gained many admirers in the 1970s and 1980s); but he failed to see the dangerously widening divergence between the two modes of human thought.[6]

Railroads As Nation-Builders

The nations that first embraced the Industrial Revolution were richly rewarded with fabulous increases in wealth and military might. Great Britain, France, Germany, the United States, Russia, and Japan were empowered by their technological and economic progress to build steel mills and munitions factories, armored ships and artillery, telegraph lines and railroads. The railroads connected the major cities of these nations as if buckling the country together with their iron tracks. Railroad lines converging in London tied Scotland to England and England to Wales, the better to keep the Kingdom united. In Russia the spokes of the railroad system reached out from Moscow in every direction, even to the Pacific port of Vladivostok. In Germany, as Bismarck unified that country, the railroad lines began to clasp Berlin to Munich, Hamburg, Strasbourg. In the United States thousands of miles of railroads linked New York to New Orleans, Chicago, San Francisco, Seattle. While physically uniting the countries that built them, railroads also helped protect the national territory. Unlike the horse cavalry (whose military role survived the end of World War I), railroad trains cannot seek out unguarded border crossings or charge through forests. Unlike the airplane, they cannot move onward without territory under friendly control. For the young nation-states of the nineteenth century, railroads were a splendid endowment received from the Industrial Revolution.[7]

At the dawn of the railroad age, empires and nations were still fragmented by the "tyranny of distance"—the time and trouble of traveling and communicating by land and sea. Until the mid-nineteenth century, people who did not live in the same village or town could not communicate with each other save by messages traveling at the speed of horses or sailing ships, journeys that might take weeks or months to reach the addressee and bring back a reply.[8] Thereafter, telegraph lines began to spread across Europe and the United States, and in 1866 even across the Atlantic Ocean. Such communications networks called for some international cooperation. In 1864 Napoleon III organized a conference among European governments to create an international telegraph system, which led to rules on codes and message routing. Political decisions were also required to synchronize time, within nations as well as worldwide. This had become urgent because the railroads, telegraph, and telephone all transcended the old mosaic of unregulated time zones. The task was accomplished by the United States and European governments between 1883 and 1912.[9]

By the end of the twentieth century, the impediment of distance for communications had been essentially eliminated, and for travel it had shrunk ten- to a hundredfold. In 1946 the cost of transatlantic air travel (economy class) was nearly ten times higher than it is today. For long-distance communications, the extra costs of spanning distance have been totally erased by the Internet and other new technologies. A map that reflects social interactions at the beginning of the twenty-first century would bear little resemblance to the natural topography of the world. If such a map were scaled to represent travel times between cities, it would shrink the whole planet into a little web resembling a road map of Western Europe. If this map were drawn to show the time (or cost) of communicating between governments, businesses, and homes it would make our world look like an ink blot.

Many scholars and pundits believe the shrinking of distance greatly enhances political and economic interactions throughout the world that are beneficial for all mankind. This might well be true for some individuals and groups—business elites, Internet entrepreneurs, nongovernmental organizations, intellectuals who embrace multiculturalism. Thus, for these sectors of society, the message of Thomas L. Friedman's book, *The*

World Is Flat, justifies its captivating title. But our world is not "flat" for nation-states that act as the ultimate arbiters of the political order and disorder on our planet. Most of these influential nations gained their strength and cohesion in the railroad age and must now cope with political problems that stem from the nineteenth and early twentieth centuries. The fought-over fragments of the Ottoman Empire—Iraq, Syria, Palestine—come to mind, or the unsettled relationship between China and Taiwan. Nothing "flat" about this world.

Widening Divergence

Ever since mankind's cultural split, science and the political order have been marching to different drummers. This divergence will widen because the scientific-technological sphere has acquired its own dynamic with which the political order cannot keep up. Nourished by an apparently unlimited succession of discoveries, science advances at an accelerating pace. Of course, scientific theories remain subject to revisions, and acquired knowledge may later be lost in the welter of competing ideas. But from decade to decade, modern science produces new knowledge and technological advances that seem destined to accumulate without end. It has become a self-sustaining force that sets it apart from all other fields of human endeavor.

No such momentum is discernible in the sphere of society, government, and international affairs. Developments in this realm travel a zigzag course, wherein improvement is often followed by deterioration, strife by pacification, rise by decline—all akin to the rhythms of history that prevailed for millennia. The power of governments grows and shrinks, their ability to control violent crime and corruption improves and deteriorates, the freedom of citizens expands and contracts, the same lessons have to be relearned from one century to the next. Man as a political animal moves on an erratic course. Man as the modern scientist moves onward, not without setbacks, but without ever changing the overall sense of direction.

Chastened by a quarter century of wars following the French Revolution, the world's leading powers—all European—created an international order in 1815 that avoided wars or kept them localized. They succeeded in maintaining this order for a hundred years. Yet after this long period of relative peace, there were two enormously destructive global wars within three decades. This phase in turn was followed by more than half a century during which wars again were averted or kept limited and localized. Manifesting a somewhat similar rhythm of gain and loss, the beginnings of constitutional democratic government in the world in the late eighteenth and early nineteenth centuries were followed, a hundred years later, by new tyrannies in Russia, Germany, and other nations. And then, after the Second World War and the end of the Cold War, these tyrannies were followed by a restoration and expansion of democracy.

Even the political enfranchisement of women, a seemingly irreversible development that began in the nineteenth century, has not followed a steady course. While it has spread all over the globe, it has suffered significant reversals recently in nations where a change of government led to the imposition of Islamic restrictions—the worst example being provided by the former Taliban regime in Afghanistan. In fact, the ups and down of religious tolerance have been an important reason for the erratic patterns of political development around the world. In some countries, diverse religious groups have lived together peacefully for generations, then suddenly became enmeshed in violence and civil war. In Bosnia, for instance, Muslims, Orthodox Christians, and Roman Catholics had enjoyed neighborly relations in the same towns and villages for generations. Then abruptly, in the 1990s, after Yugoslavia had broken up and autocratic rule was displaced by political turmoil, they started to persecute and kill each other. Something similar happened in Indonesia, where Muslims and Christians had lived peacefully in the same communities until Suharto's autocracy was replaced by democratically elected governments, at which point religious violence erupted in various parts of the country.

Economic policy and performance have followed a similar zigzag course. In the early nineteenth century, mercantilist economies steadily gave way to free market systems. Then, in the early twentieth century, the free market was partially displaced by socialist command economies. But at the end of that century, the command economies were themselves displaced by a successful global movement to restore free market economies. The course of free trade has been equally wobbly. Free trade prevailed throughout most of Europe during the last third of the nineteenth century until it ended in 1914, to be revived with the Common Market and free trade agreements forty years later. My interpretation of the divergence between the two cultural spheres—the scientific one and the ethical-religious one—is shared by John Gray, Professor of European Thought at the London School of Economics: "The belief that scientific advance engenders social progress suggests that science and ethics are alike, when in fact they are very different. Once it has been acquired and disseminated, scientific knowledge cannot now be lost; but there is no ethical or political advance that cannot be reversed."[10]

A fundamental difference between the two modes of human activity—and a source of tension between them—resides in their contrasting aspirations. In the scientific-industrial mode, human activity is devoted to a continuing progression of advances without a final goal. Science, properly pursued, does not seek to establish a definitive doctrine but to expand man's never-completed comprehension and conquest of nature. But in the societal-political sphere, people have essentially finite goals.

In Marxist thought, for instance, the communist society was not envisaged as a goal to be overtaken by some new form of capitalism. The Islamic movements that have established their theocratic states are not prepared to welcome "progress" that might lead to a religious reformation. America's policy of promoting democracy and human rights is not intended to build a transitory political order to be replaced by new autocracies.

The encyclical *Fides et Ratio*, released by Pope John Paul II in 1998, addresses this cultural divergence. The "profound unity" in Medieval thought, the encyclical notes (§45), was

> producing knowledge capable of reaching the highest form of speculation, [yet] was destroyed by systems which espoused the cause of rational knowledge sundered from faith and meant to take the place of faith.

The encyclical conveys the Pope's appeal (§48),

> that faith and philosophy recover the profound unity which allows them to stand in harmony with their nature without compromising their mutual autonomy.

At the present time, this "profound unity" does not seem within reach. Many democracies are painfully torn between the secular and the religious; and disparate faiths in the world remain deeply divided, within nations as well as between them. These irreconcilable disagreements often lead to violent conflicts which reveal—it is sad to say—the extraordinary savagery and cruelty of religious wars.

Since the eighteenth century, political leaders in Western democracies have sought to overcome these conflicts by instituting the separation of Church and State. Prominent thinkers in the nineteenth century even anticipated that the influence of religion in society would vanish. Auguste Comte, Karl Marx,

Herbert Spencer, and others portrayed the importance of religion as merely a passing phase in the evolution of mankind, to be supplanted by some universal, rationalist philosophy. Several European nations have evolved along this path. But in other regions religion became more influential and even spawned fiercely militant groups. Religious resurgence has spread through Africa, lit fires throughout the Muslim world, and can be observed in the United States.

It is mankind's destiny that its cultural split will become wider, unless the calamity of annihilation from within (see chapters 4 and 5) forces societies to close the chasm between the two modes of human activity. Short of such an upheaval, the societal and religious modes of human activity cannot catch up with the ceaseless momentum of science. This widening chasm is ominous. It might impair the social cohesion of societies, and of nations, by drawing the human psyche in two directions: to the personal and national identity that resides in acquired beliefs, memories, and traditions of the past; and to the promise of greater wealth and power offered by untrammeled technological progress. Also, mankind's two cultural spheres are driven further apart by emotions—that basic ingredient in all human activity. In the scientific sphere, we are neither emotionally tied to our cultural and religious heritage, nor pining for a final redemption. But when animated by the world's old soul, we seek to protect our identity by clinging to ancient artifacts from our ancestors and hallowed legends from the distant past.

In the 1990s, Hindus and Muslims in India killed each other in a dispute about the Babri Mosque, which is said to have displaced a Hindu temple half a millennium ago. In Jerusalem, Muslims and Jews kill and die for the Temple Mount, whose veneration by both faiths is based on even older legends. Perhaps it is our fear of mortality, that inescapable end of our earthly existence, which induces us to find solace by killing for a patrimony that has vanished long ago. A haunting thought, that Macaulay has captured:

> And how can a man die better
>   than facing fearful odds,
> For the ashes of his fathers,
> And the temples of his gods?

2

SCIENCE PUSHES US OVER THE BRINK

Men will acquire the power to alter themselves, and will inevitably use this power.

—BERTRAND RUSSELL (1931)

WE ARE AWESTRUCK by the continuing advances of science, yet often ambivalent about their impact on our world. Rightly so, because the nuclear age taught us the difficulty, nay the impossibility, of reining in threatening consequences of scientific breakthroughs. Today, it is the life sciences that keep producing successive stunners: a steady increase in longevity; therapeutic uses of stem cells; cloning of a human chimera or even a human being; new bioengineered weapons that can unleash a global pandemic; new applications of biotechnology and neurophysiology to discover the inner workings of the human brain; and eventually the ultimate leap—the construction of a superhuman intelligence—our twenty-first-century Tower of Babel.

Further progress in the life sciences seems guaranteed because the evident health benefits will assure unstinting public support. Yet the dark side of this research is now impossible to ignore. Advanced biological weapons are now seen as a major threat, and rightly so. But two emerging problems of the life sciences also deserve more scrutiny. One is the outsized cost and ethical dilemmas of the longevity expansion. We can already discern the outlines of a cramped new world in which scores of millions in developed countries are in varying stages of senescence, but could be kept alive with indefinite life-prolonging interventions that would bankrupt national budgets.

The other threatening phenomenon is harder to define with precision, though potentially far more revolutionary. It arises from the accelerating pace of research in both neuroscience and computer science, and the gradually expanding joint projects of those disciplines. Slowly coming into focus is a merger of the two versions of "intelligence"—the human brain's unique thinking ability and the computer's vast search-memory-and-computation powers. Superhuman intelligence looms on the horizon.

The Deconstruction of Death

From antiquity until yesterday, old age was not thought of as a curable affliction. *Senectus insanabilis morbus est*—old age is an incurable disease—wrote the Roman philosopher Seneca. The outer bounds of old age were understood to be the seventies and eighties, and we learn from biographies of famous people that a fair number lived that long. The Roman consul and orator Cato died at 86 in 149 B.C.; Saint Augustine died at 75, shortly after he finished writing *The City of God*; Michelangelo was creative almost until his death, a few months shy of 89; Voltaire lived to the age of 83; Benjamin Franklin lived to 84. What is new today is that a far larger proportion of people live to their eighties and often continue to participate actively in society. During the last three hundred years, most countries have experienced dramatic reductions in mortality rates. The *average* length of life almost everywhere has more than doubled, and in the developed world has tripled, rising from a norm of twenty to thirty years which had prevailed through most of recorded history.

Beyond this genuine progress lie more audacious goals. Competent experts in biotechnology now propose to transform old age into a curable disease. The "cure" they have in mind would both extend the life span and improve the quality of life in the later years. Scientists have predicted that it will become possible to extend people's active life-span by twenty years or more, probably long before the end of this century. Less clear is how many of those living longer will spend decades in senility. But even with massive uncertainties about this critical aspect, demand for the new life-prolonging treatments will be irresistible, and will confront democratic governance with agonizing choices.

A threshold question is how will decisions be made about prolonging individual lives? Physicians and hospitals play a key role in any such decisions, and medical ethics assigns a high priority to prolonging life. Even when terminally ill patients convey a preference for ending life-support measures, their wishes are often overridden. Litigation over responding to surmised wishes of comatose patients can drag on for years, in the United States as well as in many European countries. Recent disputes offer a warning of things to come. Consider the case of Terri Shiavo, a comatose woman in Florida kept alive on a feeding tube for fifteen years, until the final court decision in 2005 gave her husband permission to have the feeding tube removed. This closure was preceded by three years of court decisions and appeals, as well as legislative interventions culminating in a special bill passed hurriedly by the U.S. Congress.

Some jurisdictions have sought to clear a path through this thicket. The Netherlands legalized doctor-assisted suicide. So has the State of Oregon, but with more restrictive rules. Such laws tend to meet with strong religious opposition, although most religions make allowance for countervailing considerations. In a letter rich in beautiful passages about aging and death, Pope John Paul II reaffirmed that "the moral law allows the rejection of 'aggressive' medical treatment.'"[1] But under what conditions is a specific medical treatment "aggressive"? In the Terri Shiavo case, Catholic theologians cited a more recent statement by Pope John Paul II, asserting that providing food and water was "morally obligatory." For those guided by this precept, most of the future life-prolonging treatments might be considered "morally obligatory," especially if they turn out to be less onerous than the currently used stomach tubes and other invasive techniques.

Such treatments could also find warm support among doctors and might be eagerly requested by elderly patients. Before long, budgetary pressures would then force policymakers to limit the exploding expense of life-prolongation. It is not hard to imagine the ensuing debates. Well-intentioned theologians and ethicists would fiercely oppose any such limitations, seeing them as a "slippery slope" that leads to government-imposed euthanasia. And in case of deaths in hospitals that are now attributed simply to old age, family members supported by ethicists would accuse these hospitals of euthanasia and start innumerable lawsuits. Others will try to argue that the billions spent on life extension for centenarians ought to be used elsewhere, say to protect the lives of children who are killed in crime-ridden neighborhoods by cross-fire among drug dealers (at least one child per day in U.S. cities), or to reduce the deaths from automobile accidents (more than a hundred per day in the United States).

Still others will point to a different slippery slope. If death could be indefinitely forestalled by ever more sophisticated interventions, humanity would lose all sense of a *natural* endpoint of human life. An indefinite postponement of death would create a profound challenge for some of the major religions. The "natural" beginning and end of our earthly existence have been viewed as boundaries drawn by God—boundaries linked to the sacredness of human life. For the Christian creed, in particular, a fading of these demarcations could be more damaging than the epochal discoveries of Galileo Galilei and Charles Darwin.

Although their discoveries contradicted hallowed doctrine and centuries of teaching, they could be accommodated by adjusting peripheral aspects of doctrine. A science-driven deconstruction of the "natural" boundaries of human life would diminish a more central aspect of Christianity (as well as Islam). Also, throughout past centuries, the proximity of death for people in the prime of life has nourished the deepest sentiments of religious faiths.[2] Theologians have been rather silent on these profound problems that lie ahead.

A continuing postponement of death can also have serious fiscal implications. If democratic governments cannot raise the retirement age to compensate for our increasing longevity, they will be unable to manage the continuing growth in health care costs and retirement payments, save by cutting other expenses. Given current trends in the United States, federal spending on the elderly (Social Security, Medicare, and Medicaid) will rise from 8 percent of GDP to about 13 percent by 2030. Unless democracies can raise the retirement age, they will have to cut defense expenditures, a process that began in Europe some time ago. But given the political will to raise the retirement age gradually from 65 to 75, the workforce/retirement ratio could be stabilized or even improved—at least for the next few decades. Any serious politician knows that the retirement age will have to be raised substantially, but also knows that any such adjustment will trigger fierce opposition. In Germany, France, Italy, Israel, and other democracies, the labor unions have organized massive demonstrations against proposals for delayed retirement, often leading to street battles.[3]

Policy adjustments, when at last they are carried out, can reduce or delay a deleterious impact of technological change. But, as Yehezkel Dror pointed out, without the stimulus of a major crisis, it is difficult for democracies to make badly needed policy adjustments that are unpopular with their voters or powerful constituencies.[4] The U.S. Government passed its first major child labor law only in 1938, and the struggle to curtail

injurious child labor practices in the poorer countries has barely begun. Technological change leaves societies in a state of
maladjustment, a manifestation of mankind's cultural split. But
this predicament does not preclude governments from taking
steps, even if belatedly, to mitigate these maladjustments. To
elucidate these delayed adjustments, American sociologists—
notably Thorstein Veblen and William F. Ogburn—introduced
the concept of "cultural lag."[5] Karl Marx's idea that the bourgeoisie would produce its own gravediggers assumed it would
be incapable of closing the cultural lag with regard to organized
labor. By accepting labor unions, however, the "bourgeoisie"
did survive the "revolutionary unification" of labor that Marx
and Engels had correctly predicted. Thus the "bourgeoisie" in
the industrializing nations—except Czarist Russia—averted
the defeat that Marx had in mind for them.

Increased longevity will not only lead to fiscal problems for
many democracies but also could prolong the rule of tyrants.
Most dictators cling to power as long as possible and can command for themselves the best medical treatments. Stalin comes
to mind as a despot who would not have volunteered to retire
had his doctors been able to keep him active and fit to age 120,
and with tomorrow's medical technology he might well have
ruled his Evil Empire until 1999. Had modern biotechnology
offered Mao Ze-dong the same extended life-span, Deng Xiaop-
ing would still be waiting for an opportunity to implement his
reforms in China. Cuban exiles in Florida who are pining and
planning for a post-Castro Cuba might have to wait as Fidel
Castro anticipates to stay in power as an octogenarian.

A mistier question relates to changes in the human spirit.
During the natural life cycle that we have grown used to, our
emotional experience—of the world around us as well as of
ourselves—moves through changing seasons. In the spring-
time of youth, the emotional landscape is mottled with subtle
and flickering colors, playfully blending tones of gaiety with
quickly passing shadows of sadness. Sexual drives and feelings

shimmer throughout this delicate composition and frequently burst forth like a thunderstorm. In maturity, our emotional experience dwells longer in a single mood, and lights and shadows have harsher edges, as on a dry hot summer day. In the autumn of our lives, our feelings and sentiments become more subdued, yet are also enriched by joys and sorrows recalled from the past. And for those who can reach the last season in fair health, the sentiment of yearning—the mind's strongest grip on life—is becalmed, and eventually fades.[6] But what if biotechnology enables people to live in fairly good health much longer? What then would be the emotive melody of our journey through life? Surely, such a change in the emotions of our passage through life would alter the disposition of society as a whole. These are large questions, with elusive answers.

Who Will Control the Human Brain?

The prospect is that in the decades ahead, biotechnology—together with other sciences—may fundamentally change the human species and thus pose an elemental threat to democracy, the world order, and indeed to all civilizations. As in the past, the rights of biotech researchers to push forward on all fronts will be challenged in the name of religious and ethical principles. Today's rows over cloning and therapeutic uses of stem cells are merely preliminary skirmishes.[7] We will come to see those disputes as petty in comparison with the issue we must inevitably confront one day in the future: To what extent will biotechnology and computer science be allowed, or encouraged, to alter the innermost sanctuary of our existence, the mind that makes us human? We should not hope for meaningful international agreement on this question. Even on the far more limited proposals for regulating stem cell research, international consensus is not within reach. Should some democracies propose an international treaty to limit the permissible scope of interventions in the human brain, they will discover that several dictatorships and autocratic regimes will either reject the proposed agreement or violate it later on. Recall the appalling story of the Soviet Union's promotion of the "Soviet man," a new personality whose foremost quality is total commitment to the Communist Party.[8]

It is against this background that we must assess the continuing progress in brain sciences. Neuroscience is steadily gaining a deeper understanding of how the brain of *Homo sapiens* enables the functioning of the mind—with its intellect, will power, emotions, and mysterious consciousness. This understanding is helped along by new, noninvasive technologies that permit researchers to observe mental functions *within* the living brain. The new diagnostic tools include Functional Magnetic Resonance Imaging, Transcranial Magnetic Stimulation, and Positron Emission Tomography. They are already providing valuable data on what goes on inside the brain when it is engaged in specific mental activities. More recently, scientists have successfully used nano-sensors and fluorescent imaging to observe changes in the chemistry of individual brain-cells.[9]

Might this new knowledge point the way to enhanced human intelligence? Numerous research projects have succeeded in improving the mental faculties of animals via genetic engineering. By targeting a single gene, experiments with mice have shown measurable improvements in memory. Other experiments explored molecular processes affecting the plasticity of certain neural functions, which might show a way to limit, or reverse, age-based declines in learning. But human intelligence appears to be a polygenic trait (i.e., governed by multiple genes), and efforts to raise it substantially via genetic engineering might be difficult.[10]

Distinguished scientists have mentioned another possibility: An increase in brain size could be the catalyst to bring about decisive gains in intelligence. Among different species, and within our own species, intelligence is correlated with brain size. The brain of a chimpanzee, one of the closest precursors of *Homo sapiens*, is less than one-third the size of the human brain. During the evolution from man's primate precursors to *Homo sapiens*, some change in the genetic endowment governing brain size must have created the larger brain that now accommodates the human mind. What if it turned out that one or a few genes constituted the key to a further enlargement of the human brain, which might in turn lead to a higher level of human intelligence? This tantalizing possibility has gained support from genetic research into the cause of microcephaly (a shrunken braincase).[11]

The desire to enhance the faculties of the human mind is of course nothing new. Since antiquity, two complementary approaches have been pursued. One works directly inside the human brain, using memory drills, problem-solving practices, as well as chemical interventions, say, with caffeine or Ritalin. The other approach assists the mind from outside the body, via the senses of sight, hearing, or touch. This external approach has employed written text and ever more powerful computational aides from the abacus to the latest computers. But even as new tools were brought to the task (for example, voice tapes to memorize foreign phrases), the enhancement of human intelligence has been modest. Until the computer came along.

Computers powerfully increased the ability of the human mind to exploit immense data collections, and vastly expanded the universe that our mind can penetrate with mathematical reasoning. These enormous enhancements of the human intellect have spread to nearly every country and continue to transform all fields of science. The recent progress in DNA sequencing, for instance, would have been impossible without powerful computers. It is true, and needs to be memorialized, that scientists and engineers performed prodigies in the nineteenth and first half of the twentieth centuries using only logarithmic tables, slide rules, and cumbersome mechanical calculators.

The first powerful computers were built in the 1940s to meet demands of the Second World War, and since then the technology has graduated from vacuum tubes to transistors (in the 1950s) and silicon chips (since the1970s). It now appears nanotechnology might lead to another big step forward. The expansion of the mind's mathematical and computational tools has had an impact on civilization almost as great as the invention of writing. It is as if the human mind—by creating computer systems—has pulled itself up by its own bootstraps to higher levels of intellectual capacity.

Leading computer scientists, ever since their vacuum tube machines, expressed confidence that computers will eventually be able to do all the mind's intellectual work *without reinforcement by a living brain.* That goal, clearly, has not been reached, despite enormous advances in the science and technology of computers. But the ambitious goal has stimulated a branch of computer science, referred to as Artificial Intelligence, which developed specialized systems that can perform extraordinarily useful tasks. Signal achievements are computers that recognize and categorize patterns (fingerprints and human speech); read, store, and categorize text; perform language translations; and "learn" by adjusting to new information. Although computers do this work much faster and far more reliably than humans, they remain inferior to humans in carrying out many essential tasks—for example, developing new concepts and theories, anticipating political events, interpreting large-scale social trends.

Most computer scientists who sought to develop a machine that would rival human intelligence have used only electronic, mechanical, and other lifeless components. It is easy to see why. Unlike the squashy human brain, computers can be disassembled and put together again, their components can be altered and tested again, and the growth of their capabilities during the last fifty years has been greater than the growth of the brain's intellectual capability during hundred thousands of years. To be sure, scientists working on Artificial Intelligence seek to learn from the brain. Ray Kurzweil, an accomplished inventor of advanced types of pattern recognition, predicts that the brain will be "reverse engineered," both in its hardware and software, so as to achieve a more powerful "machine intelligence." But even this audacious approach would be hobbled by the fundamental limitations of lifeless machinery.[12]

Lifeless computers lack flexible judgment, creativity, and emotions. Emotions are an attribute of the living brain that indeed seems essential for superior intelligence. Without the diverse experience of pleasure and pain that pulsates from the living body into the brain, it has not been shown that emotions can emerge at all. Emotions impart value, and thus provide a ranking of importance to newly perceived events as well as to remembered data. By prioritizing the welter of information flowing from the brain's senses and memory, emotions help the mind in deciding what to do. Acquired and inherited emotions stored in the amygdala and hippocampus endow the human mind with a useful image and helpful understanding of the natural and social environment. Many distinguished scholars have concluded that the full intellectual powers of the mind cannot exist in a lifeless machine.[13]

Social interaction among independent minds—each with its own will, self-consciousness, and emotions—is also essential for intellectual creativity. The pervasive role of language in human intelligence is proof of that. Language can lift our thoughts and sentiments above the realm of our experience. It is the magic carpet on which our mind travels beyond the outskirts of our perceptions. It enables us to form useful thoughts about new problems or new phenomena, and is indispensable for the development of science, ethics, and religion. But language lives and evolves only through social interaction. Computers, lacking emotions, cannot have social interaction and hence must operate with language that has been preprogrammed. By contrast, the human mind, when stimulated by social interaction, expands its vocabulary and idioms to capture new concepts.[14]

So the next challenge is evident. The lifeless computer must be coupled with the inventive capabilities and judgment of the human brain—the living brain that is both the master and slave of a human body. The scientific literature has reported hundreds of disparate research projects designed to link the brain with computers. Initially, most of these projects were conducted with modest resources, and quite a few were rather playful in design and purpose. But more recently, research projects linking the brain with computers—called brain-computer interface (BCI)—have multiplied and are now being pursued at American and European universities. These BCI projects are designed to help disabled people with prostheses to move their artificial limbs, or for those missing limbs to operate a computer or other equipment with direct signals from their brain.[15] These promising projects are bound to receive increasing encouragement and financial support. Since the BCI projects serve such legitimate medical purposes and raise no ethical problems, they will proceed without provoking religious objections and risking government-imposed prohibitions on further research. And so, gradually, progress in neuroscience, biotechnology, computer sciences, and other disciplines will yield a great deal more knowledge about the triangular relationship between mind, brain, and computers.

Yet some of the best experts still seem reluctant to explore this triangular relationship as something that could be transformed into a single, integrated system. On the one hand, most studies about enhancing human intelligence remain narrowly focused on *individual* human beings—raising IQ one person at a time, so to speak. On the other, the votaries of Artificial Intelligence emphatically stress that they do not wish to smudge their clean work with the slithery brain—as if they feared contamination with mad cow disease. And neurologists and cognitive psychologists rarely invite computer scientists to help them design a symbiotic system combining computers and human brainpower, apart from the therapeutic brain-computer links to help disabled people.[16] Such delimiting of different scientific disciplines is more common now because of the growing complexity and richness of each branch of science. Yet from time to time, bridges get built between different disciplines that bring sudden, great advances.

As night follows day, enterprising scientists will build such a bridge between computer-based Artificial Intelligence and brain science. They will begin to organize interdisciplinary projects to integrate computer systems with the mental power of living brains. Their ambitious aim will be to reach a level of intelligence well above the human range. At this time, no one can describe all the theoretical and technical problems that have to be solved for the project to be started in earnest, and it would likely require an effort with generous financing and strong support by many scientists—neither of which is available today. But at some uncertain date in the future, the search for this superhuman intelligence will become a major priority of the world's leading countries. This will happen when it sinks in that superhuman intelligence really might be attained, and that its attainment would revolutionize all prior considerations about national security.

If U.S. intelligence organizations discovered that a nation with strong scientific capabilities—for example, China—had made significant breakthroughs on such a project, government support for a competing project in the United States would suddenly become available. Recall that America's expensive project for the manned mission to the moon—something for which there had previously been little enthusiasm—easily garnered Congressional support when it appeared that the Soviet Union was about to accomplish the feat. Recall also that the fear Nazi Germany might acquire the atomic bomb (although in the event unwarranted) triggered the U.S. decision to launch the Manhattan Project, at the time an immense and uncertain venture.

At the start of that project, none of the physicists involved could have described the full research and development program which produced the atomic bomb three years later.

A competitive race with China to build the first super-intelligent system might start sooner than most think tanks and government forecasters expect. And also sooner than I had expected when I wrote a first draft of these pages three years ago. Since then, Chinese scientists and institutes of the Chinese Academy of Sciences have published numerous articles about an "integrated" large facility for linking a brain trust and computers to work on complex policy issues. It seems this project is meant to draw on brain science and computer science (Artificial Intelligence) to combine human intelligence with high-performance computers. I am indebted to Michael Pillsbury for his insightful and knowledgeable assessment of these Chinese projects.[17]

Could such a two-nation race for achieving a super-intelligence system lead to the construction and actual use of an integrated brain-computer system, and a subsequent strategic competition between two or more national systems? I have not seen a good case made that such a system could not be developed before the end of this century. Its purpose would be greatly to enrich and expand what advanced computers can do by creating a symbiosis between, on one side, a computer system designed for this purpose, and on the other side, the judgmental capacities and essential emotive functions of the human brain. The contribution of the living human brain would probably not come from one individual "hooked up" to a computer, but from computer linkages to an expert committee or group of policy advisors. Such a symbiosis would be far more advanced than the latest brain-computer links.

If successful, this new intelligence system would exceed the intellectual performance of the best expert group. It would integrate human minds with the enormous memories and calculating and organizing capacities of advanced computers. If and when such a well-financed and focused project achieves its first demonstrable success, the door will be opened to a fundamental transformation of human civilization. In my judgment, the greatest, most profound transformation of the human condition will not derive from the prolongation of life, or from the anxiously debated—and probably vastly overrated—possibilities of human cloning and "designer babies." Instead, I see an effective synthesis of the computer with living human brains as the agent that will lead to a truly revolutionary upheaval for the human race.

What is at stake in any such synthesis is an increase in intelligence comparable to the step from primates to *Homo sapiens*. The obstacles to our comprehension of such a world are fundamental, and in the last analysis perhaps insurmountable. We can no more imagine the political order of this new world than a group of chimpanzees in the forest can comprehend what goes on among humans in a nearby village. Whether we should welcome or oppose any such transformation is one of those philosophical questions to which a crisp answer seems impossible. As Ludwig Wittgenstein put it: "Whereof one cannot speak, one must remain silent."

The idea that a national project might construct an effective super-intelligent system cannot be dismissed as science fiction. This prospect is thrust forward by at least two forces—the continuing progress of brain science (which is widely supported to find cures for brain-related diseases), and the steady advances in computers (which are fueled by the ambitions of powerful corporations). Although progress today is most visible in the United States, we cannot assume that America would prevail over a future adversary in a race to develop this super-intelligence. Despite America's strength in computer science and brain science, it would have some disadvantages in any such race. One would be the constraints on research imposed by ethical and religious considerations. In the past, neuroscientists have gained critical knowledge by studying patients with major brain injuries. At some stage in the project's development, a nation's research might greatly benefit from intrusive experiments on living human brains. Liberal democracies would normally shun such experiments, but ruthless dictatorships would not.

A related but potentially more important inhibition in America would derive from ethical and religious objections to the very pursuit of superhuman intelligence. This might limit the participation of some of America's best scientists. The legions of ethicists now worried about cloning would suddenly discover they had focused on the wrong issue. Religious organizations would come to regard the quest for a super-intelligence as the ultimate threat to their faith and doctrine—and rightly so. Thus a two-country competition to build the first superhuman intelligence system could turn into a race the most ruthless nation would win.

In Western democracies there would surely be urgent demands that the development of this system be controlled by the United Nations: to "make it legally binding" that it be used only for benign, peaceful purposes, "for the benefit of mankind." Anyone predisposed to think this might be a feasible policy—a policy that could truly be implemented and enforced—would do well to review the history of biological weapons or to recall the lessons of the nuclear age.

Bio-weapons and Politically Correct Illusions

The most frequently mentioned dark side of the life sciences is their misuse to enhance the lethality of biological weapons. A rich literature is now available on this threat, so I need not dwell on it at great length. The biological weapons that have been used sporadically in the past employed naturally occurring pathogens or toxins—bubonic plague, anthrax, botulism, and many others. Sometimes the effectiveness of these natural agents has been increased—for instance, by converting anthrax spores into an aerosol form. But in the future, a nation or a terrorist organization could employ genetically engineered agents that are far more lethal than natural ones, or that have been made resistant to all currently available vaccines and remedial medications. To unleash an epidemic, a small amount of such an agent would suffice and could be delivered clandestinely—hidden in a bottle, a fountain pen, or pillbox. Add to this threat the possibility that the terrorist might "reload" his means of attack. As former Secretary of the Navy Richard Danzig correctly points out: "Biological terrorism affords the possibility of repeated attack, undermining confidence and forcing ever-escalating investments of resources to achieve a modicum of defense."[18] These frightening prospects prompt people to call for international agreements to ban such weapons.

Unfortunately, the history of arms control is disfigured by an ever-expanding list of broken treaties. So we must expect that international agreements will at best provide only partial protection. On a few occasions, to be sure, a treaty might have kept a vicious dictator from using prohibited bio-weapons; but because he feared retaliation, not because he wanted to be law-abiding. The treaty, in essence, drew a red line that the dictator hesitated to cross. Thus, the Geneva Protocol of 1925 (a one-page treaty banning the first use of poison gas and biological weapons) might have reinforced Adolf Hitler's hesitation to risk the kind of poison gas warfare he himself had witnessed in World War I.

In 1969 President Nixon ordered the destruction of U.S. biological weapons, and two years later he submitted to the Senate the new convention prohibiting the production and stockpiling of bio-weapons. Peripheral issues delayed ratification until 1974, when it became my job as Director of the Arms Control and Disarmament Agency to urge the Senate Foreign Relations Committee to consent to this BW Convention. I warned the senators up-front that "verification of compliance with this

convention in countries with relatively closed societies is difficult." After a couple of minutes' discussion, the senators nonetheless agreed the Convention should be ratified. Yet later on,
the Convention's unverifiability became a nagging issue. In the
1990s it was discovered that the Soviet Union had massively
violated the Convention from the first day it signed it. And after
Saddam Hussein had lost the Gulf War in 1991, he was also
forced to admit to massive violations.

To assess what arms agreements can do to prevent bio-
warfare, we need to keep in mind the "dual use" problem. It
makes detection well-nigh impossible in authoritarian nations
and dictatorships—precisely the countries where violations are
most likely to take place. Advances in the life sciences spread
throughout the world because, almost without exception, they
are intended for peaceful uses. But the boundaries between
destructive and beneficial purposes are easily blurred. For instance, a new pharmaceutical vector that helps to transmit a
medication to the diseased tissue might be indistinguishable,
for practical purposes, from vectors that can be used to magnify
the lethality of a biological weapon. The very fact that one of
the two uses is beneficial, and hence considered humanitarian,
would make it politically difficult to impose stringent controls
on the worldwide transfer of such pharmaceutical vectors.

Unfortunately, the BW Convention offers little protection because biological weapons can be developed under the guise of
peaceful use and are easy to deliver clandestinely. At least two
signatories of the Convention—the Soviet Union and Iraq—admitted that they violated it. In 1992, Russia's President Boris
Yeltsin revealed that the Soviet Union has been developing biological weapons, an illicit program that apparently started right
after Moscow had signed the Convention. In 1995, when the
head of Iraq's military industries defected, Saddam Hussein was
forced to admit his massive violations of the Convention. Obliv-
ious to these stubborn facts, the UN arms control conference

in Geneva was tasked to write a new treaty, a "Protocol" to the BW Convention that would deter such violations.

By 2001, when this Protocol had grown 200 pages long, the Bush administration called a halt to the negotiations. The diplomats who had enjoyed their many pleasant sojourns in Geneva understandably reacted with outrage and insisted the negotiations had to be resumed. Less understandable was their rationale for negotiating this Protocol. It would be "legally binding," they explained, and therefore effective. But if a dictator is willing to violate the BW Convention—presumably also a legally binding treaty—why on earth would he suddenly feel "legally bound" not to violate this Protocol as well? Evidently, as long as an illusion is politically correct it remains impervious to logic and evidence.

3

FIVE LESSONS OF THE NUCLEAR AGE

Those who've governed America throughout the nuclear age and we who govern it today have had to recognize that a nuclear war cannot be won and must never be fought.

—RONALD REAGAN (1982)

THE DRAMA OF THE NUCLEAR AGE teaches painful lessons. The continuing spread of nuclear technology is turning into a disaster of unimaginable proportions. It is moving beyond the control of any national policy or international agreements. It is the quintessential expression of mankind's cultural split—the inability of institutions to rein in runaway science. How did we get pulled into this awful maelstrom? Specifically, how has the United States, originally the possessor of a nuclear monopoly, ended up facing a crisis of extreme vulnerability, a world where ruthless dictators, terrorist organizations, even doomsday cults and anarchists can some day possess a few nuclear bombs?

Eleven American presidents—from Harry S. Truman to George W. Bush—tried to prevent this from happening. At the beginning, the United States assumed the principal responsibility for the nuclear question, appropriately so since it emerged from the Second World War as the strongest power and the only nation that had built and used atomic bombs. Since then, Americans have devoted an immense effort to the nuclear problem—an intellectual, political, and military endeavor that has no parallel in all of military history. As a longtime participant in this effort, both inside and outside the Pentagon, I feel free to state that much of it took the form of an abstract and cold-blooded theorizing of an eerily academic nature. Nonetheless, when all is said, a stellar accomplishment spans the entire period from 1945 to date. Nuclear war, and indeed any destructive use of nuclear bombs, has been averted.

Lesson One: Benevolence Is Not Enough

Drawing the most useful lessons from the nuclear age will require immersion in the rich and complex history of the last sixty years. I shall select only the most instructive episodes, but to convey the essence I need to start at the beginning.

During the Second World War, public opinion had become inured to devastating bombing attacks on cities—until the nuclear destruction of Hiroshima and Nagasaki. That event thrust a new emotive impulse upon strategic thinkers everywhere. Just one single bomb, oh Lord, could now destroy a major city! The wrenching revelation that one of nature's most powerful forces had been unlocked slashed like a flaming sword into people's consciousness, prompting statesmen and military leaders to search out a new approach to war and peace. For months to come, a flow of information deepened the emotive impact of the atomic bomb: first the gruesome photographs, then harrowing tales from survivors, later a series of studies by scientists working for U.S. and Japanese authorities. What endowed these clinical reports with political salience were the tales of human victims—of instantly incinerated neighborhoods, of skin burned off the living flesh, of strange and fatal illnesses. The enormity of this unfolding story gripped the moral imagination of people throughout the world.

I want to stress here the link between witnessing the human impact of the atomic bomb and the will to act boldly in forestalling nuclear warfare. The emotional experience of a dramatic, real-life event is a far more potent motivator for choosing an audacious policy, or a benevolent policy, than are theoretical forecasts. During the first year after the A-bomb attacks on Japan, such emotional hindsight emboldened leading statesmen, hard-nosed politicians, and military strategists to seek an unprecedented transformation of the international order. It was as if the sudden emotional comprehension had inspired them to seek salvation through a generous offer for total reform.

Consider Dean Acheson, whose views were expressed in a memorandum for President Truman six weeks after Hiroshima. Acheson, bear in mind, was no woolly-eyed disarmer; a couple of years later he was to lead the effort to create the Atlantic Alliance as a bulwark against Soviet expansion. Yet in September 1945, this tough-minded, illusionless policymaker wrote for his equally tough-minded political master that nuclear weaponry was "a discovery more revolutionary than the invention of the wheel," and that "if the invention is developed and used destructively there will be no victor and there may be no civilization remaining." He recommended approaching the Soviet Union to explore international controls for a global ban on nuclear weapons. British Prime Minister Clement Attlee was even more anxious to stop further development of atomic bombs. In a handwritten memorandum in the fall of 1945, he noted that "the only hope for the world is that we should . . . strive without reservation to bring about an international relationship in which war is entirely ruled out."[1] He was not alone in that belief.

By November, U.S.-British discussions had led to a remarkable decision: International controls of nuclear weapons must be a responsibility of the United Nations—a still untested organization. To develop a U.S. position, Truman established a committee chaired by Dean Acheson, and its conclusions (which became known as the Acheson-Lilienthal report) called for an international authority that would confine the use of atomic energy entirely to peaceful purposes. This benevolent idea gained the support of leading nuclear scientists, including (it is worth noting) Edward Teller, the famed physicist who became one of the principal proponents and a key inventor of thermonuclear weapons. Teller called the report "the first ray of hope that the problem of international control can, actually, be solved."[2]

This was truly a wondrous episode in the history of nations. At a time when only the world's most powerful nation could have produced these weapons, it sought instead a radical, yet generous solution—to prevent all countries, *itself included*, from working on nuclear weaponry. To monitor this universal self-denial, the international authority advocated by Acheson-Lilienthal would have been given "exclusive jurisdiction to conduct all intrinsically dangerous operations [regarding nuclear materials]."[3] How could this amazing episode have taken place? A major reason was the advice given by the atom bomb's creators. America's nuclear scientists justifiably enjoyed enormous prestige after their extraordinary accomplishment became known in August 1945. Although they had their differences, the scientists agreed on three forecasts, all absolutely essential for the President of the United States to bear in mind: first, that the information necessary to design nuclear weapons would not long remain an American secret; second, that the Soviet Union and several other countries would build their own nuclear bombs in the not-too-distant future unless constrained by a new international regime; and third, that it would become possible for advanced industrial nations to build nuclear weapons vastly more destructive than the first atomic bombs. Within a decade, all three of these forecasts had been proven correct.

Scientific forecasts are rarely sufficient to bring about a fundamental innovation in the political sphere, no matter how clamant the predicted problem. It was clearly the searing experience—history's first destruction of a city by a single bomb—that made possible America's gamble on nuclear policy in the autumn of 1945. Without the emotionally reinforced forecast, Washington would almost certainly have regarded its monopoly on nuclear weapons as an asset to be tucked away.

Within six months after Hiroshima, the well-intentioned project to restrict nuclear technology to peaceful uses had reached a dead end. As policymakers in the West had feared, Soviet opposition blocked all progress.[4] The Soviet Union conducted its first test of an atomic bomb in 1949, and in 1950 North Korea's attack on South Korea led to a huge expansion of the U.S. and the Soviet nuclear arsenals. The fading of "emotional hindsight" during the second half of the twentieth century goes a long way to explain the horrendous accumulation of nuclear weapons and the perversities of nuclear strategy.

Lesson Two: "Deterrence" Was Oversold

Mercifully, the ever more menacing volcano remained dormant. After August 1945, the only nuclear weapons detonated were for testing, and after 1962 even tests became rather furtive, most of them hidden deep underground. Without new pictures of the mushroom cloud, the world grew accustomed to nuclear nonuse. Many strategic thinkers attribute the nonuse during the Cold War to mutual deterrence between East and West. But if one reexamines the evolution of nuclear doctrine and deployments, as well as the growing size of the nuclear arsenals and the responses to major crises, it becomes clear that the explanation is more complicated.

An enormous literature on deterrence has been written—top-secret government reports, public testimony for Congress, thousands of books and articles. As noted by Robert Jervis (himself a creative contributor to this field): "many of the best ideas [on nuclear strategy] are old and . . . not all of the new ideas are good." That many of the best ideas are old is confirmed by an article written four months after Hiroshima. At that early date, Jacob Viner explained essentially all the benefits and problems of deterrence, and anticipated with astonishing foresight and beautiful clarity the transformation of international affairs that nuclear proliferation would cause. Since then, nuclear strategists became more and more fixated on "deterrence" as if it were a concrete, empirically observable entity. The American philosopher Alfred North Whitehead called such an excessive reliance on an abstraction "the fallacy of misplaced concreteness."[5]

"Deterrence" theorizing postulates how a "potential" aggressor calculates whether to attack—a hypothesis hard to test empirically. By contrast, the nonuse of nuclear weapons is not a hypothesis; it has been evident since 1945. Indeed, it has prevailed *even in wars that nuclear-armed powers have lost against non-nuclear nations.* By the end of the Cold War, many strategists came to see nonuse and deterrence as two sides of the same coin: nonuse became the proof of successful "deterrence" and "deterrence" the strategy guaranteeing nonuse. Alas, 9/11 casts anguishing doubts on this proposition.

Since war never broke out in Central Europe during the forty years when the largest military confrontation in history divided the continent, it is tempting to assume nuclear deterrence preserved the peace. This view remains unproven; Soviet archival documents released so far do not provide an answer. It is, however, unquestionable that America's nuclear superiority did *not* keep the peace on the Korean peninsula. Released Soviet documents confirm that Stalin authorized Kim Il Sung (the North Korean dictator) to attack South Korea in June 1950, although the United States had some 350 atomic bombs at that time and the Soviet Union only about five. Stalin even remained undeterred after the United States had come to the defense of South Korea: he supported North Korea with Soviet fighter pilots. Had nuclear superiority really been effective in deterring aggression, the United States would not have suffered 33,000 fatalities and 92,000 wounded in defending South Korea against North Korea and China, neither of which had nuclear weapons at the time. Nor was this the only occasion on which nuclear-armed nations have accepted stalemate or defeat in wars with enemies that did not have a single nuclear bomb. The United States did so in Vietnam, the Soviet Union in Afghanistan, and in 1979 a nuclear-armed China withdrew from its cross-border aggression into Vietnam. Then there is the case of the 1962 Cuban missile crisis. It would be a fallacy of misplaced concreteness to believe that nuclear deterrence safely prevented war on that occasion. That crisis was caused by the Soviet Union's provocative deployment of nuclear missiles in Cuba and nearly triggered a full-scale, yet unintended nuclear war.[6] Let us note, Cuba 1962 was not a crisis that could have been prevented by the "deterrent" effect of nuclear weapons—it was *caused by* nuclear weapons.

Lesson Three: We Were Lucky—So Far

Deterrence can ward off only deliberate attacks, it cannot dissuade an accident from happening or a madman from detonating a nuclear bomb. The world seems to have been close to an accidental nuclear war during the Cuban missile crisis, as well as on several less visible occasions. What averted the accidental Armageddon? Was it the prudence of all those managing the nuclear arsenals, was it the intervention of extraordinary good luck, or—seen in a transcendental way—the intervention of Providence?

I shall open the problem of accidental nuclear war by describing my own professional encounters with it. During the 1950s, I worked at the RAND Corporation, a think tank in Santa Monica, California. That decade was RAND's most creative period—a time when its scientists, sustained by generous contracts with the Air Force, could pursue a range of innovative ideas. Many of us at RAND worked on nuclear strategy, elucidating the need for survivable retaliatory forces, credible response options, and other critical issues. Much of our thinking was recorded only in top-secret documents. Then, one morning in March 1955, the newspapers brought us Winston Churchill's grand speech on deterrence (his last major speech in the House of Commons). I recall vividly our astonishment at RAND that day. Here the British Prime Minister had expressed all the key ideas of our secret work—and with such eloquence! Who had authorized him to go public?

In any event, I felt the workings of deterrence were becoming a rather crowded field of inquiry, and that it might be more useful to explore the possibility of a nuclear catastrophe that deterrence could not prevent. Might a nuclear weapon be detonated accidentally, or a missile launched because of an unauthorized act? With the help of RAND's weapons experts, I was able to demonstrate that in many situations just one person (with authorized access) could trigger an unauthorized detonation, either "by accident" or "by design"—however much the design was conceived in madness. Together with Gerald Aronson, a brilliant psychiatrist who consulted for RAND, I reviewed then-current procedures for selecting personnel with access to nuclear weapons, as well as medical statistics on the occurrence and types of dangerous mental disorders among active military personnel. Aronson and I concluded that existing personnel procedures could not prevent mentally unstable individuals from gaining access to nuclear controls. Special personnel screening would help, we suggested, but it could not guarantee complete protection. Hence our recommendation: that two people always be in charge of the truly critical controls, and that coded safety locks be placed on all weapons and missiles exposed to the risk of unauthorized launch.

RAND endorsed these findings, and I was sent to Washington to brief a sizable audience of Air Force generals. As a young researcher at my first high-level Pentagon briefing, I delivered my rather simple message with trembling knees. But the next day, General Curtis LeMay, then Vice Chief of the Air Force, had heard about my study and asked for it. General LeMay is justly famous for having built the U.S. Strategic Air Command into the world's most formidable nuclear deterrent; yet he also became known for his injudicious pugnacity regarding the use of nuclear weapons. We at RAND expected him to oppose locks that might slow down *his* use of *his* weapons. Yet we learned that LeMay had commanded a blizzard of actions. He ordered the Air Force to adopt our recommended personnel screening procedures and the two-man rule for critical nodes. He also urged the nuclear laboratories to work on the coded locks we advocated, and prompted the Army, Navy, and Defense Department installations to take similar steps. My memory insists on placing this experience in the "success" column of my life's ledger.[7]

The unauthorized use of nuclear weapons is not the only way in which a cataclysm might be initiated by accident. Although the United States deployed thousands of nuclear missiles that could be launched almost instantly—in a single salvo—some influential missile experts feared the enemy could destroy our whole force before it got off the ground. Accordingly, they urged that the "retaliatory" salvo ought to be launched upon receipt of warning that an enemy attack had been started—the "warning" in this case being an interpretation of radar screens and perhaps other signals that an attack *appeared* to be on its way. Many advocates of this perilous "launch-on-warning" policy misrepresented it as arms control. They argued that the United States and Soviet Union would be condemned to an indefinite arms race unless the situation was "stabilized" by threats of *mutual assured destruction*—which became known as MAD—meaning each side could instantly inflict devastating retaliation and thus always deter an attack.[8]

The doctrine held that (1) defenses against missiles had to be banned lest they prevent retaliation, and (2) each side had to keep its missiles poised for instantaneous launch lest they might be destroyed on the ground. This double-barreled position—"yes" to launch-on-warning, "no" to missile defense—became the accepted dogma for quite a few liberal politicians.[9] I am convinced both ideas are deeply flawed.

At the time these arguments were gaining currency, I was Director of the U.S. Arms Control and Disarmament Agency (1973–1976) and could use my inside-the-government position to stress the danger of launch-on-warning. Shortly before President Nixon nominated me to head the agency, I had published an article on this danger.[10] (The article almost cost me Senate confirmation because it had somewhat unflatteringly quoted an endorsement of launch-on-warning by Senator William Fulbright, then chairman of the Foreign Relations Committee.) I had further encounters with this issue when I served President Ronald Reagan as Undersecretary of Defense for Policy from 1981 till 1988. One of my areas of responsibility in support of Defense Secretary Weinberger was nuclear strategy. During those years in the Pentagon, I learned a good deal more about the far-flung U.S. command-and-launch system and its complex interactions with what the Soviets were doing. Bruce Blair has written compelling warnings about these risks of accidental nuclear war.[11] I was appalled to learn how close the Carter administration came to relying on launch-on-warning procedures as an acceptable way to make mutual deterrence more "stable." And I became more convinced than ever that my earlier condemnation of launch-on-warning was prescient.

We must keep in mind that this dangerous Cold War legacy is still with us: highly destructive U.S. and Russian missiles remain capable of being launched within minutes. Over the years, there have been false U.S. radar signals indicating a Soviet nuclear attack, errors in the use of critical computers (illustrated by the mistaken Pentagon warning in 1980 of an incoming Soviet missile attack), and more hidden problems of unauthorized acts. Dangers have surfaced even from routine maintenance procedures (illustrated by the Chernobyl accident). In 1995, a bizarre incident occurred in Moscow when President Boris Yeltsin reacted with public bluster to an innocent Norwegian missile used for weather research.

Lastly, there is a persistent disconnect between, on the one hand, the specialists who know how to design and maintain different nuclear weapon systems, and on the other, the authority to examine the overall system in its entirety and, if needed, to order remedial action. The few most senior officials who would have the authority to look into every facet of this far-flung system have neither the time nor technical understanding to do so. But a review commission of subordinates large enough to include all the required expertise is unlikely to get full access to every piece of this secretive domain. To my knowledge, the various commissions tasked to conduct a "complete" review could never get to the bottom of all serious problems. The members either were not given access to, or were not told about, this or that arcane risk. For example, applying locks on missile launch controls or on the detonation mechanism of weapons is a frequently praised safety measure (which my 1958 RAND study had first recommended). These locks—it is said reassuringly—can only be opened with a numeric code that is available to no one but to the highest national authority. In reality, however, these codes have to be installed and maintained by many technicians, some of whom might inadvertently, or deliberately, leave some weapons or missiles unlocked. So far, luck has been with us.

Lesson Four: What Reagan Taught

Ronald Reagan had a different philosophy about the nuclear peril: he was deeply troubled by the risk of mistakes or accidents that could lead to Armageddon. I was a foreign policy advisor in his election campaigns (from pre-primary to the final campaign), and in July 1979 I participated in a small meeting that my friend Richard V. Allen had arranged with Reagan to review nuclear strategy. As we addressed the vulnerability of our missile forces to Soviet attack, Reagan heard us out patiently and then remarked that an acquaintance of his (whom I knew as a frantic industry executive) had told him there was no vulnerability problem at all—we could simply launch our missiles as soon as we had warning of an attack. Reagan paused briefly to let the point sink in (while I anxiously held my breath) and then added with firm conviction: "But I think, this is the wrong thing to do!" He had made my day.[12]

Reagan's judgment on this issue was not a casual reaction. It reflected an understanding of nuclear weapons that was at once realistic and humane. His views contrasted favorably with the self-proclaimed expertise of many defense intellectuals who are prone to what Alfred North Whitehead called "the fallacy of misplaced concreteness." The same philosophical underpinnings explain Reagan's decision—taken over the objection of the State Department—to endorse Weinberger's recommendation that we seek a U.S.-Soviet agreement to get rid of *all* intermediate nuclear missiles deployed in Eastern and Western Europe. The State Department wanted to negotiate a lower, common level for these missiles that would—in the euphemism of mutual deterrence theory—"stabilize" a new nuclear confrontation between East and West. Reagan liked the idea of eliminating all these new missiles. As Weinberger later wrote: "Contrary to virtually all of the popular myths about him" Reagan "actually was very unhappy with the need to rely on nuclear weapons. . . . All of the required briefings, exercises, and the 'Doomsday' scenarios new Presidents have to be given, simply reinforced his own beliefs."[13] The proposal to reduce both the Soviet and the U.S. intermediate range missiles to zero was Richard Perle's idea. He served as Assistant Secretary of Defense during most of the years when I served as Undersecretary of Defense for Policy, and he managed NATO affairs and arms control issues with brilliant inspiration and hard-knuckled bureaucratic skills. Would that more Americans willing to serve in government possessed both Perle's creative intellect and his ability to translate good ideas into effective government policies.

It may seem counterintuitive, but I believe that one must be something of a wimp to endorse a confrontation of missile forces primed, day and night, year after year, to execute mutual genocide. Failure to grasp the magnitude of this gamble betokens a lack of emotional strength. No one can be certain that any such "mutual deterrent" will never fail. Fortunately, Reagan understood that reliance on the mutual nuclear threat was "a sad commentary on the human condition," and with his Strategic Defense Initiative of March 23, 1983, he boldly swept aside decades of mistaken theorizing. He reached this decision knowing the arguments on both sides of the issue, thanks to his many discussions during his presidential campaign. His chief foreign policy advisor Richard V. Allen had organized these tutorials, expertly gathering the best strategic thinkers representing a wide range of views.

Yet it took another eighteen years for Washington and Moscow to overcome the doctrine of Mutual Assured Destruction. The catalyst for change was George W. Bush's decision in 2001 to withdraw from the treaty banning missile defenses—a move that infuriated diehard supporters of MAD thinking. But George W. Bush and Vladimir Putin realized that the genocidal implications of MAD would harm useful cooperative relations between their two nations, and President Putin understood this better than the European and American arms control aficionados. They firmly predicted that ending this treaty would force Russia to expand its missile force, and almost felt betrayed by Putin when he did no such thing.

Reagan was not the first conservative statesman to distrust the concept of mutual deterrence. Winston Churchill had strongly supported America's initial nuclear advantage in the fall of 1945, when he was the leader of the opposition.

But by 1953 the Eisenhower administration's apparent insouciance about putting atomic weapons "to military use" deeply troubled Churchill (who had again become Prime Minister).[14] Even more important in reshaping Churchill's thinking at that time was the impact, emotional and intellectual, of the recent thermonuclear weapon tests. On March 1, 1954, after the Soviet Union had demonstrated that it could build a thermonuclear bomb, the U.S. test at Bikini Atoll in the Pacific resulted in a yield of 15 megatons (equivalent to fifteen *million* times the largest conventional bombs of World War II), and—unforeseen by the designers of that test—spread radioactive contamination over the ocean that would have been fatal to unprotected people within an area of some 7,000 square miles.

Churchill, who always prided himself on his careful attention to scientific knowledge, was particularly moved by the data on the power of thermonuclear bombs made public by the chairman of the U.S. Atomic Energy Committee. He wrote to Eisenhower on March 9: "You can imagine what my thoughts are about London. I am told several million people would certainly be obliterated by . . . the latest H-bombs." He urged Eisenhower to agree to a U.S.-British summit meeting with the new Soviet leaders, a proposal he had already made after Stalin's death the year before. Eisenhower remained opposed, and with hindsight one might judge him right since no great opportunity for arms control was missed at that time. Only after Gorbachev had revolutionized the political thinking in the Kremlin could Reagan and George H. W. Bush reach agreements with the Soviet Union to eliminate whole classes of nuclear weapons.

It must be granted, though, that Churchill's timing made some sense. The Soviet leaders, too, had changed their views of nuclear war. It appears that even Communist dictators could be moved by the emotional impact of H-bomb tests. Before 1954, the Kremlin held to the thesis of the "inevitability of war" between East and West. Twelve days after the 1954 American H-bomb test, Georgii Malenkov, the new Chairman of the Soviet

Council of Ministers, made a statement opposing "the policy [*read*: Stalin's policy] of preparing [for] a new world war, which with modern weapons means the end of civilization."[15]

I see these reactions by government leaders as another instance of emotional hindsight emboldening foresight—giving statesmen the courage and foresight to fear nuclear weapons. A personal experience can strengthen this courage. Churchill had suffered a stroke less than a year before his letter to Eisenhower, and surely knew that he was close to the end of his career. This might have illuminated for him, with transcendent clarity, the reasons for the shallow public reaction to the searing facts about the thermonuclear bomb. As he put it:

> The reason is that human minds recoil from the realization of such facts. The people, including the well-informed, can only gape and console themselves with the reflection that death comes to all anyhow, sometime. This merciful numbness cannot be enjoyed by the few men upon whom the supreme responsibility falls. They have to drive their minds forward into these hideous and deadly spheres of thought. All the things happening now put together, added to all the material things that ever happened, are scarcely more important to the human race.[16]

Lesson Five: Beware of "Peaceful Use"

The Cold War bequeathed the world a frightening detritus: thousands of nuclear weapons and tons of fissile material suitable for making bombs—mainly in the United States and in Russia. Because of Moscow's fiscal and administrative turbulence, control of Russia's inherited detritus is of special concern. To safeguard it, the United States and European nations have provided assistance for a cooperative program with Russia, a farsighted effort conceived and initiated in 1991 by Senators Sam Nunn and Richard Lugar.[17]

But leftover Cold War weapons are not the only curse that technologies of mass destruction have placed on mankind. The know-how and wherewithal to make atomic bombs is spreading to more and more countries, including some of the worst dictatorships—and is likely to spread beyond the control of national governments. Endlessly aggravating this process is the "curse of dual use": the fact that many of the most destructive technologies also have innocent, peaceful purposes, which provide the cover and excuse for dispersing them hither and yon.

As if hexed by a mischievous fate, arms control initiatives meant to limit the proliferation of weapons technology have themselves turned into agents accelerating proliferation. There is an echo of Greek tragedy in this phenomenon. In *Oedipus Rex*, Sophocles' finest Greek drama, the parents of Oedipus sought to escape the horrible prophesied fate by contriving a frantic scheme to defeat the prophecy. Yet precisely that scheme became the means—almost the only possible means—to make the prophecy come true. Since the 1950s, the Oedipus tragedy has played out before the world's uncomprehending gaze: multilateral agreements meant to control dual-use nuclear technologies have worked instead to further weapons proliferation.

The tragic course of events can be traced back to the Atoms for Peace program launched by President Eisenhower in 1953. It was meant to enlist international support for curbing the spread of the atom bomb by offering peaceful benefits of atomic energy to the world at large. Yet countries that were offered an agreement to receive technological assistance exclusively for peaceful uses managed to create loopholes enabling them to divert the assistance to their nuclear weapons program. As in the Oedipus tragedy, capricious developments made the prophesized fate come true. Henry Sokolski's book, *Best of Intentions*, offers striking evidence of the errors that drove the United States to spread nuclear assistance so generously without insisting on tight controls. The generally hard-nosed John Foster Dulles and Lewis Strauss (Chairman of the Atomic Energy Commission) ordered the U.S. negotiators to accept with minimal restrictions the demands of India and other countries that wished to receive nuclear technology. By yielding to nations that wanted the agreement made easier to cheat—India comes to mind— the United States demonstrated lack of conviction in opposing nuclear proliferation. The Cold War prism through which U.S. officials viewed the perils of proliferation aggravated this weak negotiating strategy. Senior officials believed in the 1960s that America's interests would only be threatened if a nation could amass a vast stockpile of weapons, enough to destroy the United States.[18] We have since learned otherwise. This history of how competent officials can become trapped in a mistaken, yet well-intentioned policy ought to be compulsory reading for all who believe international agreements are the way to control the dark side of technological progress.

No other U.S. policy, no multilateral policy, no United Nations activity has done more harm than the Atoms for Peace program in hastening and expanding the spread of nuclear know-how for building bombs. And once the United States had legitimized the worldwide transfer of nuclear reactors, England, Canada, France, Germany, Japan, and the Soviet Union began to compete with the American exports. Reactors, either for "research" or for electric power, were thrust upon less-developed countries all over the globe, and these gifts enabled the recipients to acquire nuclear materials and know-how. The recipients included Iraq, North Korea, Iran, Vietnam, Yugoslavia, the Congo, and even Laos. In recent years, we have witnessed a "multiplier effect" of this largesse. China has helped Pakistan to build nuclear bombs, and the developer of Pakistan's bomb, Abdul Qadeer Khan, has helped North Korea, Libya, Iran, and possibly others with their nuclear weapons program. It is far too late now to close these loopholes of the nuclear Nonproliferation Treaty. The treaty mandates a review conference every five years, but despite the growing concern about nuclear proliferation, the month-long review held in May 2005 ended in failure.

This is not the end of the Oedipus tragedy. Throughout the world, plutonium accumulating as waste from nuclear power reactors, or excess left from weapons programs, has become a troublesome product whose cost of disposition, as Richard Garwin puts it well, "is greater than the value to anyone who might buy it—except to those who want to make nuclear weapons."[19] The authorities responsible for nuclear energy in Russia, the United States, and other nations have been trying to find a way out of this disastrous situation. They are promoting projects that would let the countries with accumulated plutonium "waste" make the plutonium safer and at the same time squeeze economic value out of it.

The leading proposal now is to recycle the plutonium and mix it with uranium, a mixture called MOX that can be used to fuel power reactors. Yet while the MOX is being shipped to the reactors its plutonium could still be extracted. In fact, that extraction would be easier than obtaining plutonium by reprocessing spent reactor fuel. North Korea, let us note, asserts that it has mastered some time ago the more difficult reprocessing of spent reactor fuel to build bombs. A safer fuel-mix (the Urex-Plus fuel) is supposed to be ready within five years and would gradually replace MOX. But a dictatorship that receives Urex-Plus fuel for its power reactors could acquire the know-how to extract plutonium from this fuel to build bombs, particularly if it coerces its technicians to do their work despite being exposed to high levels of radiation. It seems we will experience a second coming of the Atoms for Peace project. More and more countries will demand nuclear power reactors, citing their "inalienable right" granted by the Nonproliferation Treaty "to develop research, production and use of nuclear energy for peaceful purposes." Almost inevitably, the spread of reactors and fuel-deliveries to every corner of the globe will enlarge the number of countries capable of starting an illicit bomb-making program.

Plutonium is an element that essentially did not exist on our planet. Only human ingenuity and the intense conflicts between powerful nations have created this element in such huge amounts. And once created, we cannot make it go away. What an emblematic predicament of mankind's Faustian bargain! For six decades, statesmen, strategists, and arms control experts have tried, and tried again, to control the spread of nuclear weapons. Now we begin to realize that our attempts to escape the predicted calamity have helped bring it about—Sophocles' *Oedipus* writ large. A sad ending of good intentions. Ineffably sad.

4

ANNIHILATION FROM WITHIN

If you keep gazing into an abyss, the abyss will gaze back into you.

—FRIEDRICH NIETZSCHE

The beginning of wisdom is fear.

—MIGUEL DE UNAMUNO

THE FALL OF THE ROMAN EMPIRE did not empower ruthless cults or crazed anarchists to extirpate law and order in every province of the realm. But such an unprecedented reign of violence might become mankind's fate in this century. The ineluctable dissemination of technology and scientific discoveries will make nuclear and biological weapons accessible to merciless insurgent movements, small terrorist gangs, secretive anarchist groups, and genocidal doomsday cults. Although some scholars and officials have warned of this peril, nobody so far has gazed into this deep abyss.

During the last few years, the media has published frightening news, based on confirmed events as well as credible rumors, about jihadist terrorists trying to obtain a nuclear bomb. One shudders to think what our enemies could do, should they succeed in this quest. They might manage to smuggle the bomb into an American or European city and cause a cataclysm beyond all telling. Dozens of writers have published gripping stories about such a calamity.[1] But their stories usually end before the morning after the nuclear destruction and ignore the ensuing long-term upheaval that would engulf our whole planet like a global tsunami.

If we keep gazing into this abyss, we burden our psyche with disquieting thoughts. As Nietzsche warned, the abyss will gaze back into us. Yet fear is the beginning of wisdom. I shall now try to shed some light into this world of darkness, a world that will confront all nations with security threats they have never faced before.

Neglecting Defensive Measures

The recent waves of terrorism confound our strategic planners more than the proverbial fog of war. Overawed by the boldness and skill of the 9/11 attack, military experts have come to interpret the tactics used by militant Muslims as if they were a new form of warfare. Yet these attacks—always stealthy and often indiscriminate—are much like the tactics that have been employed in protracted insurgency wars (as in Chechnya or Sri Lanka), or that have been used to exert political pressure and gain attention (as by the Red Brigade in Italy or the Palestinian Intifada). It is also worth recalling that the use of stealth and surprise is a time-honored stratagem. Stealthy attacks by disguised fighters served Allied war aims in World War II, a tactic that was known as "sabotage." The bravest Allied fighters carried out dangerous sabotage attacks on military targets in Nazi-occupied territories, especially France and Norway. One might argue that such stealthy attacks in World War II had been preceded by a declaration of war and therefore should not be likened to "terrorist" attacks.[2] At which point an annoying critic will interject that the only declared war since then has been Osama bin Laden's jihad.

America's military planners have fought terrorist tactics primarily with offensive measures, sometimes to the neglect

of complementary defenses. Many successful offensive operations have been carried out since 9/11, above all the defeat of
the Taliban regime in Afghanistan. As if to justify an exclusive reliance on offensive warfare, we keep condemning the
ruthlessness and immorality of stealthy attacks. With laudable
compassion and a somewhat maudlin mien, we describe our
civilian victims of such attacks routinely as "innocent." In fair-
ness, shouldn't we keep in mind that our *combatant* victims are
just as innocent? It was our neglect of defensive measures that
made it easy for the enemy in 1983 to launch the deadly assault
on the U.S. Marine barracks in Beirut; and again in 1996 to
bomb the U.S. military quarters in the Khobar Towers in Saudi
Arabia; and again in 2000 to launch a shaped charge into the
destroyer USS *Cole*. Oddly, we blamed each of these disasters on
the "cowardly" sneak attacks of terrorists. We scarcely blamed
the tragic losses on the shameful failure to defend our *military*
assets and our *military combatants*—whether they are resting in
their quarters or on full alert.

The idea that "offense is the best defense" remains popular among U.S. military officers and their civilian leaders, perhaps because of America's past experience. During its entire
history, the United States has been attacked within its territory
only three times: in 1812, 1941, and 2001. So we continue to tell
ourselves that the best way to fend off attacks on the 9/11 model
is to go after the terrorists in their lairs and "bring them to jus-
tice." Clearly, to achieve an effective offense-defense synergy we
must carry out offensive strikes against aggressors who are preparing to attack us, as well as against organizations that support
these aggressors. As Secretary of Defense Donald Rumsfeld
correctly pointed out, terrorists have an advantage: they "can
attack at any time, in any place, using virtually any technique."
And since the United States cannot defend against all these potential attacks, it has become accepted U.S. policy to pursue the
war on terrorism abroad. The object, Rumsfeld explained, is "to
go after them where they live and plan and hide, and to make

clear to states that sponsor and harbor them that such actions will have consequences." As President George W. Bush put it: "We are fighting the enemy in Iraq and Afghanistan and across the world so we do not have to face them here at home."[3]

Now the time has come to look beyond today's familiar threats: Al Qaeda and other jihadist terrorists, Iran's growing nuclear capabilities, North Korean nuclear bombs. Although these contemporary problems have not yet gone away, the United States, other democracies, and indeed most nations ought to prepare themselves to cope with a new, potentially more overwhelming form of aggression. Nations will have to prevail against an attack that seeks to annihilate their political order from within. My next chapter will address how we might cope with this new challenge; but first I shall explain its insidious progression and nearly unstoppable force.

Dark Warnings

Within the next half century, perhaps even within a decade or two, a nation might be vanquished—not by a foreign terrorist organization or by the military strength of a foreign power, but by a small group of domestic evildoers ruthlessly using weapons of mass destruction against their own country. This grim prospect is not new. We were told about it quite some time ago.

Theodore B. Taylor, who worked at the Los Alamos National Laboratory as a nuclear physicist, wrote a memorandum in 1966 entitled "Notes on Criminal and Terrorist Uses of Nuclear Explosives." He warned, "I am becoming increasingly concerned that not enough attention has been given to the possible ways by which a few people that have a very small number of nuclear explosives can . . . cause violent disruption of human activities on a national, or even international scale." Taylor discussed several compelling scenarios and added that "the group [that would use these nuclear explosives] need not be identifiable with any organization against which the U.S. could retaliate." Among recent assessments of such covert attacks, a usefully comprehensive one is the book *America's Achilles' Heel* by Richard A. Falkenrath, Robert D. Newman, and Bradley A. Thayer.[4]

In 1973, when I became Director of the U.S. Arms Control and Disarmament Agency, Taylor's warnings spurred me to have my staff review the danger of poorly guarded nuclear materials. One problem that caught our attention was the fuel used in research reactors that the United States had donated to dozens of countries. Incredibly, the fuel the U.S. Government provided was highly enriched uranium (HEU)—the ideal material for making bombs. I tried to have the safer, low-enriched uranium substituted; but the U.S. agency that provided this dangerous fuel (a predecessor of the Department of Energy) failed to take action. Only recently has the United States begun to retrieve this dangerous uranium—at, alas, a maddeningly slow pace.[5] On this issue, as on so many others, policy initiatives to control dangerous technologies can easily be defeated by hidebound bureaucrats and parochial technicians.

We also must not forget that in the fall of 2001, someone in the United States obtained anthrax spores (in the aerosol form suitable for biological warfare) and sent deadly amounts by U.S. mail to members of Congress and other addressees, thus causing more than a dozen fatalities plus huge cleanup costs. Actually, had this quantity and quality of anthrax been employed more effectively, it could have done far greater damage. It might have shut down the nationwide mail systems. Despite an intensive, prolonged search by the FBI, the "someone" could not be found. Over four years, FBI agents and postal inspectors have pursued leads on four continents and conducted more than 8,000 interviews.[6] It appears that this advanced biological warfare agent was obtained *within* the United States, and without the assistance of a foreign government. Several types of mass destruction weapons can be manufactured at home without help from abroad. In 1995, entirely on Japan's territory and undetected by the normally competent Japanese police, chemists belonging to the Japanese doomsday cult Aum Shinrikyo manufactured the poison gas sarin—a rather complex task.

These episodes offer heavy hints about our future—about a time when criminal dissident groups or cults can employ weapons of mass destruction against a nation without the support of a rogue state and without any need of a hideout in a failed state. Even if the perpetrators required some technological assistance from another country, the foreign source need not present the attacked nation with suitable targets for retaliation. In the late 1970s and early 1980s, the Irish Republican Army (IRA) received the hard-to-detect Semtex explosive through Libyan diplomatic pouches. Libya did not suffer British retaliation, even though the British government had been struggling to put an end to IRA attacks in Ulster and England for more than a quarter century. The IRA also received money and arms from sympathizers in the United States, the better to commit acts of terrorism against the British government. Her Majesty's Government did not deem a retaliatory strike against these American suppliers a viable option. Or consider the guilt of Dr. A. Q. Khan, the founder and longtime leader of Pakistan's nuclear weapons program. When the U.S. Government learned that he had provided designs for building nuclear weapons as well as material assistance to Libya, North Korea, Iran, and perhaps other countries, the United States neither carried out a retaliatory strike against Pakistan nor tried to kill Dr. A. Q. Khan, who still lives comfortably in Pakistan.[7]

Let us admit it, we have had no end of a lesson: anthrax in the United States, sarin in Japan, a Pakistani mail-order business for nuclear weapons components, scientific papers on the Internet explaining how to engineer lethal viruses. We can hear

the distant thunder, we can see the dark clouds, we feel the chill
in the air that precedes the approaching storm, and yet we are
grasping for reasons to deny what our knowledge is telling us.

The Anarchists' Return

The "curse of dual-use technologies" will become a growing
predicament for all democracies—indeed, for all nations that
want to be part of a peaceful international order. As I have noted
in chapter 2, genetic engineering, molecular biology, and other
life sciences serve valuable peaceful purposes, as do several
applications of nuclear technology. Yet all these great achievements can be misused to build weapons of mass destruction, in
some cases with but minor modifications.

Exploiting dual use to inflict immense injury on a society is
not a new idea. The nineteenth-century anarchists had thought
of it. As documented in Walter Laqueur's magisterial history of
terrorism, the International Anarchist Congress of 1881 passed
a resolution that its affiliated organizations and individuals
ought to learn about the most deadly weapons by studying
chemistry and other technologies. At that time, the anarchists
also gleefully welcomed Alfred Nobel's invention of dynamite,
expecting that it would empower them to destroy the political
order they wished to erase.[8] It turned out dynamite was not destructive enough, although the anarchists amply demonstrated
that they had the necessary ruthlessness. Between 1880 and
1914, they killed U.S. President McKinley, assassinated over a
dozen European prime ministers, and killed many other senior
statesmen. What they lacked were the necessary tools. Now, in
the twenty-first century, they will have the tools to pursue their
ambition in ways far more consequential than the assassina-
tion of McKinley in 1901 by anarchist Leon Czolgosz.

Anarchists and doomsday cults are likely to attack their own country from within, not from abroad. They want to create havoc in their homeland and may not care about preserving the wealth and strength of their nation. Like Karl Marx's proletarians, they believe they "have nothing to lose but their chains. They have a world to win." Although today's anarchists and leaders of doomsday cults can obtain far more destructive weapons than dynamite, few will have the strategic brilliance and political cunning to win in their country, let alone "to win the world."

The lack of a winning strategy is well illustrated by Shoko Asahara, the founder and leader of the Japanese cult Aum Shinrikyo. Shoko Asahara gained the world's attention in 1995 when his followers released the poison gas sarin in Tokyo's subway. The attack injured some 6,000 people, in addition to killing 12 subway passengers. As a manager, Asahara was astonishingly effective and successful. He built up a global organization with assets worth several hundred million dollars and a scientific-technical staff competent enough secretly to manufacture sarin. Yet his strategic thinking was utterly vacuous. He fantasized that he could cause some kind of Armageddon in Japan and then miraculously impose his cultist state on Japan, or perhaps on the whole world. This story conveys a significant point: The fact that a cult leader possesses the charisma to recruit technically competent followers who can build weapons of mass destruction does not mean he has the savvy to lead his cult to victory.

But another aspect of the story is troubling. Precisely because his goals were so nebulous, Asahara found it relatively easy to recruit and retain well-educated followers. The renowned Japanese novelist Haruki Murakami watched Asahara's followers in their court trials and interviewed several of them. He found that the cult members, looking back at the crime in which they had participated, repeatedly praised Asahara's "correctness of aims." He had won their hearts and minds by letting them hitch their

own well-meaning private fantasies to his vague pronounce-
ments about "the five races living in harmony" or "the whole
world living under one roof." What the technicians and scientists working for Asahara had in common, Murakami concluded, "was a desire to put the technological skill and knowledge
they had acquired in the service of a more meaningful goal."9
This is a cautionary tale for those who contentedly assume democracies will be able to control the dark side of science.

Biological agents might be the weapon of choice for anarchists. In one of the many biotechnology laboratories at universities or pharmaceutical research institutes, a technically
qualified member of an anarchist group could divert peaceful
applications to create weapons. And since anarchists, in essence,
want to create chaos to destroy the existing order, they need not
fret about the unpredictability of untested biological agents. By
contrast, a Muslim organization that wants to resurrect the caliphate would be ill-advised to use infectious bio-weapons. By
starting a global pandemic, they could cause a boomerang effect that would kill far more Muslims than "infidels."

How would a small gang of anarchists or one of the doomsday cults want to use a biological weapon? An attractive target
would be a summit meeting that brings together many presidents and prime ministers. In recent years, the annual G-8
meetings that gather the leaders of rich and powerful nations
have been a favorite target for rowdy demonstrators. Their purpose has been to accuse the wealthy nations of some misdeed
and attract media attention with their ranting and chanting.
But a twenty-first-century anarchist who made it to the gates
of a G-8 summit with a powerful biological agent would have
more in mind. He would seek to incapacitate, or kill, the entire political leadership of the world's most influential nations.
Just one such attack, if successful, would inflict great damage
on international relations. Keep in mind, a biological agent
that is being smuggled into a building is far more difficult to

detect than a nuclear bomb. Hence, all future meetings among senior officials would have to adopt massive security measures that would constrain international diplomacy and cramp democratic practices.

Moreover, there is a threshold of civilian deaths and destruction beyond which even the most stalwart society begins to malfunction. Detailed studies from World War II provide empirical data regarding this threshold. British and American air raids routinely attacked urban residential areas in Germany and Japan, not only because they were easier to hit than military targets but because it was assumed that killing civilians would usefully damage "the morale" of the enemy society. At the end of that war, the U.S. Government conducted a survey to assess the effectiveness of these "morale attacks." The survey found merit in a distinction, introduced by Nazi authorities, between the mood (*Stimmung*) of the inhabitants in the bombed cities and their deportment (*Haltung*). If "morale" was gauged by people's deportment rather than their mood, the bombing of urban residential areas in World War II—whether in Germany, England, or Japan—did not reach the threshold to be to be strategically effective.[10]

Similarly, Osama bin Laden's extraordinarily skillful surprise attack of September 11 darkened the mood of Americans with shock, anger, and even a touch of mawkish self-pity (some Americans plaintively asking: "Why do they hate us so much?"). But the attack did not reach the threshold that would have weakened the deportment of Americans. On the contrary, it made the United States somewhat stronger. For many years before 9/11, government experts and high-level commissions knew full well what ought to be done to prevent terrorists from hijacking an airplane. Yet nothing was done to implement their recommendations until the body politic responded to the horrific image of the collapsing World Trade Center, the multiple airplane crashes, and the casualties. Osama bin Laden raised

America's defenses against terrorist tactics to a level that the U.S. Government, left to itself, could not reach.

"What does not kill me makes me stronger." Friedrich Nietzsche's apothegm captures a rugged truth.

A Nuclear Power-Grab

The cause of freedom would not have advanced so far but for the strategic folly of the enemies of democracy. "The good news from history is that attackers often fail to win the wars that they start with stunning surprises," noted Richard Betts, Professor of War and Peace Studies at Columbia University.[11] This is also true of terrorist attacks. Walter Laqueur's exhaustive studies of the subject led him to conclude that "in most cases, terrorism, in the longer run, made no political difference one way or another—in some, it caused the exact opposite of what the terrorists hoped and intended to achieve."[12] Terrorist leaders often have the most nebulous strategic goals, or more often, no achievable strategic goals at all. Like many other aggressors, they lack a grand strategy and are prone to strategic folly. The greatest danger for the international order in this century will be the emergence of an aspiring dictator who is utterly ruthless, brilliantly cunning, and possessed of strategic vision. This malignant combination has been exceedingly rare in the past, and we have no reason to fear it will now be more frequent. What will be altogether different in the decades ahead is that such an adversary can gain access to weapons of mass destruction.

Perhaps the most relevant historic parallel is Lenin's power grab in St. Petersburg, in November 1917. With his ruthlessness and extraordinary strategic smartness, Lenin exploited the chaos in post-Czarist Russia to impose his Bolshevik dictatorship.

The First World War had dissolved the Czarist armed forces, torn apart the social order in Russia's countryside, and fractured the civil society in Russia's capital. This political destruction enabled Lenin to wrest dictatorial power from the short-lived Provisional Government which had replaced Czarist rule in Russia. Aleksandr Kerensky, who presided over that liberal-socialist government, wrote that the word "revolution" was an understatement for what had happened in Russia: "A whole world of national and political relationships sank to the bottom, and at once all existing political and tactical programs, however bold and well conceived, appeared hanging aimlessly and uselessly in space."[13]

The First World War was the wrecking ball and sledgehammer that cleared the site for building the Bolshevik regime. A future Lenin need not wait for a third world war to create a social wasteland on which to impose his new tyranny. A few nuclear weapons will do just as well.

But physical destruction by itself, even on a large scale, will not empower the would-be dictator to rule the ravaged country. In the 1990s, Slobodan Milosevic's violent marauders surely broke apart multiethnic Yugoslavia, but in 2002 Milosevic's political career ended in the jail of the International Criminal Tribunal in The Hague, where he died four years later. Pol Pot annihilated the existing regime in Cambodia and inflicted immense casualties throughout the country, but in the end he was driven from power to hide in the jungle where he died a reviled murderer. To achieve a more lasting victory, the aspiring dictator would likely use a stratagem that Leon Trotsky called "dual power." This stratagem is "the historic preparation of a revolution," according to Trotsky, and it played a critical role in Lenin's takeover. For decades since then, it has been used by Communists trying to get a foothold in the West while remaining loyal to Moscow.

As Trotsky explained the concept:

The political mechanism of revolution [or in my story here, the mechanism of a "nuclear power-grab"] consists of the transfer of power from one class to another. The forcible overthrow is usually accomplished in a brief time. But no historic class lifts itself . . . to a position of rulership suddenly in one night, even though a night of revolution. . . . The historic preparation of the revolution brings about in the pre-revolutionary period a situation in which the class which is called to realize the new social system, although not yet master of the country, has actually concentrated in its hands a significant share of the state power, while the official apparatus of the government is still in the hands of the old lords. That is the initial dual power in every revolution.[14]

To make the dual-power stratagem more relevant for our time, replace Trotsky's out-of-date expression "old lords" by "incumbent leadership," and "the class called to realize the new system" by "dictator's followers." Thus the stratagem simply means that the aspiring dictator implants some of his political followers in the incumbent government—for example, by forming his own legitimate party that gains a minority status in the parliament. Meanwhile, his more brawny followers can be trained to help with the forcible overthrow of the incumbent government.

Successful dictators have spent years on the preparatory campaign to build up (in Trotsky's words) "the class which is called to realize the new social system," or put in contemporary language, to build a movement of followers and a political party that can win votes. For Lenin the preparatory campaign started in the 1890s, when he gained an influential position in the clandestine Russian Social Democratic Labor Party. At the Second Congress of that party, in Brussels in 1903, he created his Bolshevik faction, a more militant organization that he led and inspired until his return to Russia in April 1917. By that time, generous German financial assistance enabled him to create a legitimate party press, as well as an illicit network of Bolshevik cells ready to use violence.[15] Thus the Bolsheviks, as a minority party in the First All-Russian Congress of Soviets, concentrated in their hands a significant share of the state power of Russia's Provisional Government. At the same time, Lenin strengthened his network of illicit military detachments for the forcible overthrow of the government that his followers had infiltrated.[16]

For Hitler, the political phase started in 1920, when he became the leader of the new National Socialist Party. He then wrote and propagated *Mein Kampf*, and gained an ever larger following thanks to his powerful oratory. He promoted an ideology that appealed to German nationalism, and also exploited the widespread anti-Semitism in Germany as a rabble-rousing theme to stimulate hatred and violence useful for his campaign. Although the economic crisis of the Weimar Republic in the end helped Hitler to seize power, his charisma among masses of Germans had deeper roots. He was a relentless and effective campaigner well before he achieved total power. On a single day in 1932, for example, he gave speeches in Aachen, Cologne, Frankfurt, and Wiesbaden. He appealed to a lower-middle class that felt politically neglected; he articulated the social anxieties of this class; and he evoked enthusiasm with the histrionics and pageantry that the Nazis so ably displayed.[17] He was thus able to gain a strong, *legitimate* foothold in the parliament of the Weimar Republic, while retaining control over his storm troopers so competent in using violence. Then the Reichstag fire (more on which below) gave Hitler a double assist. First, it offered a political and legal pretext for Hitler to grab total power; and second, it created a psychological crisis among the German people that made them accept Hitler's power grab. In the event of a *nuclear* power-grab, the extreme national security crisis of a sudden nuclear detonation would provide legal justification for the new leader to declare emergency powers, and the profound emotional shock would make the people inclined to tolerate the emergency rule.

It is prudent to remember not only the horror of Hitler's well-known abominations but also the danger of his political-psychological skills that carried him from victory to victory—from 1932 until 1941. Only late in 1941 did Hitler's strategic folly emerge, first in his conduct of the campaign against the Soviet Union following the German army's Blitzkrieg advances to the outskirts of Moscow and Leningrad, and shortly thereafter Hitler's absolutely fatal mistake—the unnecessary declaration of war against the United States.

The dual-power stratagem has been widely used by insurgents and terrorist organizations. It has been used by the Basques, who fomented terror attacks to seek independence from Spain but also established a legitimate political party, Batasuna, allegedly independent of the Basque terrorist organization ETA (Euskadi Ta Askatasuna, or "Basque Country and Freedom" in Basque language). The Spanish government tolerated this duplicitous game for many years until in 2002 it finally outlawed the Batasuna Party. That decision has since been criticized by many European newspapers as "undemocratic." In Ulster, Sinn Fein continues to function as a legal political party allegedly independent of the Irish Republican Army (the militant IRA feared for its terrorist acts). Sinn Fein has successfully cast itself as a peaceful political movement opposed to terrorism but sympathetic to some of the "just" goals of the IRA. It has made itself the principal interlocutor with the British Government. The well-known connections between the IRA and Sinn Fein have hardly spoiled this "dual-power stratagem." It is no secret in Ireland, England, and the United States that Sinn Fein's leader Gerry Adams belonged to the IRA in the past and had been in charge of the Belfast IRA operations at a time when its units killed fourteen soldiers as well as civilians.[18] Adams refused to condemn several IRA bombings that caused grievous casualties, yet his party obtained millions of dollars in private contributions from well-meaning Americans who want Ulster to be fully independent of London, in a unified Eire. The dual-power stratagem (backed by conventional explosives) might yet work for Sinn Fein, if it is willing and strong enough to maintain a compromise settlement, and if both camps in Ulster can convince their extremists to end the use of violence.

The availability of nuclear weapons, of course, would transform the dual-power stratagem. The aspiring dictator could prepare to employ two or three nuclear weapons for maximum political impact, without mounting a military campaign across national borders and without support by another nation or by a foreign terrorist organization. He would not provide the attacked nation any targets for a counterattack. He would thus render useless the most advanced offensive weapons and the most powerful nuclear deterrent forces of the victimized nation. He would heed Machiavelli's advice: "Any harm you do to man should be done in such a way that you need not fear his revenge." He would seem to be nowhere and everywhere.

He might have his nuclear bombs smuggled into the nation he plans to attack, or he might have them assembled within that nation. To employ the weapons, he could use a single two-man sabotage team, which would be nearly impossible to detect with the means available to a democratic government (unless it had an effective system of sensors, an issue I shall address in the next chapter). The two members of this team would have to be totally loyal to the aspiring dictator, and compulsively secretive. Once in possession of a couple of nuclear bombs, they would never have to think about becoming suicide bombers, they would never need any flight training, and to deploy their bombs properly they would not have to reconnoiter the target and thereby risk being detected. They could transport the nuclear bomb in a harmless-looking van, park it legally in the center of the city to be destroyed, trigger the detonation from a safe distance, and thus conveniently melt down their fingerprints, the automobile license, and all other evidence. After the first nuclear detonation, the aspiring dictator would rely mainly on his legitimate organizations and his popular influence to seize political power by exploiting the chaos, havoc, and psychological shock he had deliberately caused.

Many nondemocratic governments will be more vulnerable to a nuclear power-grab than well-established democracies. For example, authoritarian leaders of Central Asian republics seek to avert the establishment of fundamentalist Islamic societies. Yet a more fundamentalist religious order is favored by large and well-organized population groups in these countries and might gain the support of the majority. In Uzbekistan, Turkmenistan, and Tajikistan, over 80 percent of the population are Muslim. One nuclear bomb detonated in the country's capital could eliminate the authoritarian leader and much of his power structure. This awful shock might enable a militant religious leader to mobilize his followers and seize control of the nation. In Iraq the young cleric Muqtada al-Sadr recently demonstrated that a skillful and assertive Muslim leader can rapidly gain a dominant political role.

In Russia, a successful nuclear power-grab would cause an immense international crisis, given its size, cultural importance, economic weight, and above all its large nuclear arsenal. The chronic insurgencies in the North Caucasus region—well within Russia's borders—could be a seedbed for Muslim terrorism. In addition, Russia's messianic cults (such as the White Brotherhood) and political extremist groups (such as the National Bolshevik Party) might come under the spell of a leader who wants to carry out a nuclear power-grab.[19]

To attempt a nuclear power-grab in a well-established democracy would require different tactics. In the dual-power stratagem the aspiring dictator would have built up his the lawful political role by propagating a seemingly benign new ideology that appeals to youthful groups, to the nation's underclass, and to leaderless activists thirsting to be recognized as an emerging political force. He would have to be half-witted—and hence unsuccessful in the end—if he tried to campaign on jihadist themes, or on "neo-Nazi" themes in the manner of those European politicians of the far right who manage to attract huge counterdemonstrations against themselves. Instead he might seek to recruit followers among restless minorities. In a West European nation the minority of choice could be disaffected youths among second-generation Muslims, in the United States it could be illegal Hispanic immigrants or unassimilated legal ones. But initially, an aspiring dictator attempting a nuclear power-grab might present himself as a compassionate, liberal "antiracist" who cares about the welfare of *all* minorities.

He would make sure that any organization with which he is openly connected is perfectly legal. To this end, he might build up his own political party, or start a faction within one of the major existing parties. He could also establish a think tank, the better to collect all sorts of information openly and to disseminate sophisticated propaganda. He would thus gain influence within the legitimate political establishment as a candidate prime minister (or president). When a critical election approaches in which the incumbent leader campaigns to be reelected, the aspiring dictator would promise more effective policies to avert a clandestine terrorist attack with a nuclear weapon.

Then, when the election date is near, he would order his two henchmen to detonate one of the low-yield nuclear bombs, perhaps in the capital. Television and radio networks would instantly converge on the aspiring dictator as the candidate who had warned against precisely this attack. Now a recognized candidate, he would gain nationwide publicity. As soon as he wins the election—or even if he can only assert that he won by exploiting the uncertainties of an utterly chaotic vote-count—he will order his "Heinrich Himmler" or his "Feliks Dzerzhinski" to organize a secret police skillful in the use of violence to intimidate political opponents. In 1918, Lenin had Dzerzhinski staff his secret police with Latvians and other foreigners. In the same manner, the new dictator, to consolidate his nuclear power-grab, might staff his secret police partly with thugs and assassins who had been trained by one of the foreign narcotics cartels. This devilish gambit might help him stir up hatred against minorities and thus create a despairing, divided society—people whom a brutal tyrant can easily rule. In this grim new world, democracies would be at risk everywhere.

Could the United States become the victim of an aspiring dictator employing nuclear violence cloaked in deception? *It Can't Happen Here* is the title of Sinclair Lewis's political fiction published in 1935. It portrays a Fascist senator who promises easy solutions to overcome the Great Depression, and who ends up winning the presidential election of 1936. The story line has the new president gaining total control of the U.S. Government, in a sequence somewhat analogous to Hitler's coup in 1933. Once elected, the Fascist president employs paramilitary storm troopers for the essential acts of violence.[20]

The truth is that in the 1930s—before the age of nuclear weapons—this really could not have "happened here." Despite the hardship of the Great Depression, the American people would have upheld their democratic traditions and constitutional government.

Likewise today, the United States would be the most difficult target for any such nuclear power-grab, not because of its superior military might or its elaborate homeland defenses (which leave much to be desired anyhow), but because of its inner political strength. Yet this political strength would melt away if America's broken immigration policies could not be repaired and continued to let mass immigration overwhelm America's capacity for assimilating its new arrivals. The historian Arthur M. Schlesinger Jr. has warned of the "disuniting of America" and explained why multiculturalism is not the answer. "The bonds of cohesion in our society are sufficiently fragile," he wrote, "that it makes no sense to strain them by encouraging and exalting cultural and linguistic apartheid."[21]

The Tidal Wave

After a stealthy attack on a city with a nuclear bomb, anthrax, or sarin, those responsible are likely to remain unknown for some time, while a charismatic leader might then succeed in grabbing dictatorial power. Whether or not this leader instigated the attack, his opponents will accuse him of having done so. The story of Hitler and the Reichstag fire offers an example. In the night of February 27, 1933, barely a month after Hitler had been appointed Chancellor of the Weimar Republic, the Reichstag building in Berlin was destroyed by a fire. At that time, Hitler had not yet consolidated his dictatorship. With great political cunning, he immediately exploited the dramatic conflagration by accusing the Communists of having caused it to launch a Bolshevik revolution in Germany. This political offensive enabled Hitler to declare a state of emergency, based upon which he rapidly entrenched his rule of terror and violence. Not surprisingly, many foreign commentators at that time assumed the Nazis themselves had burned the Reichstag building to give Hitler the pretext for his power grab. Since then, however, some respected historians have disputed the charge, and the culpability for the Reichstag arson remains unsettled to this day.[22]

As Americans have learned from the anthrax attacks in 2001, uncertainty about the perpetrator feeds rumors and political dissension. After a nuclear bomb had stealthily been used to destroy the heart of a major city while the government could not provide a convincing identification of the perpetrators, the people would start to mistrust their government. Some might seek consolation in pseudo-religious fantasies, perhaps convincing themselves that the Apocalyptic time of the Rapture had arrived and that the incumbent government is the Antichrist. But the tide of angst and uncertainty will also have serious international consequences. In every nation with a functioning government, the leaders and political elites will begin to fear their country might be next. Moreover, the sudden end of nuclear nonuse—a universal dispensation that has lasted since 1945—could ignite a rapid, further proliferation of nuclear weapons. If the victimized nation is a major nuclear power, it is likely to alert its strategic forces for preempting a possible follow-on attack, this time by a foreign enemy. Other nuclear powers would discover the alert and alert their own nuclear forces. Such a many-sided interlock of forces that are being mobilized recalls the calamity of August 1914. If the nuclear power-grab occurred in Pakistan, many Pakistani's would blame India for having provided the bomb or actually employed it; and vice versa, if the clandestine detonation occurred in India.

We also know from history that even the best and the brightest often lose their moral compass during times of war or during periods when nations fear a devastating surprise attack. The confrontation with wanton carnage, deception, and cruelty summons the Furies of revenge, who can convert peace-loving, liberal-minded elites into promoters of genocide. During World War II, J. Robert Oppenheimer, who frequently articulated ethical values that resonated with liberals, wanted to spray Strontium 90 (a baleful carcinogenic element) on Germany. According to Joseph Rotblatt (a nuclear scientist from the era of the Manhattan Project), Oppenheimer wrote in 1943 to Enrico Fermi, who was in charge of the first reactor in Chicago, that he should not begin the project until he could produce enough Sr-90 to kill half a million people. During John F. Kennedy's presidency, the U.S. war plans for retaliation in the event of a Soviet nuclear attack provided for targeting millions of people in the hapless captive nations of Soviet-controlled Eastern Europe (which would have fiercely opposed the Soviet attack, given a chance). And the Kennedy era war plan would also have China instantly targeted, even though it might not have been involved in the Soviet attack.[23]

Although 9/11 changed international affairs significantly, it left the basic architecture of the world order intact. This will not be the case after an anarchist cult or an aspiring dictator has made effective use of one or a few weapons of mass destruction. The political and military leadership of all nations would not take long to recognize they face an entirely new kind of enemy, a deadly force that nations have never before experienced. How could the world order be restored after a well-established nation suddenly had been annihilated from within?

There is nothing now discernible on the geopolitical landscape to prevent such an attack from happening—save, perhaps, an unending continuance of good luck. We do not know how to build a citadel to protect democracies from nuclear or biological weapons. We do not know how to create a world order that would truly remove these monster weapons as a threat to mankind. And thus far, at least, we lack the resolve to plan ahead. Unless we give this awesome prospect some serious thought, we will be without a strategy to deal with it and without the tools to prevail.

It is high time to get serious.

5

TIME TO GET SERIOUS

If we lose faith in ourselves, in our capacity to guide and govern, if we lose our will to live, then indeed our story is told.

—WINSTON CHURCHILL (APRIL 24, 1933)

OUR CAPACITY TO GUIDE AND GOVERN WILL BE indispensable if we are to survive the coming era of proliferating mass destruction weapons. Few strategic planners are aware of the ultimate finality of a nuclear or biological attack from within. And none have yet braved the difficulties of planning for it. Understandably, our political leadership is preoccupied with immediate security problems that clamor for prompt attention. Our intelligence services focus on hostile remnants of Al Qaeda, newly emerging jihadist groups, turmoil and killings in Iraq, a continuing danger of terrorist attacks in Indonesia, Afghanistan, Madrid, London, Jordan, the United States. It is the disasters we have recently experienced that make similar dangers real and fearsome. More distant perils ahead seem like a blurry specter, beyond the horizon of our emotions.

So we brush the troublesome forewarnings aside. We dismiss from our mind the fact that many current and future technologies can be misused for mass destruction; that such technologies continue to spread across borders as well as inside our national territory; that this proliferation is essentially irremediable; that evildoers keep trying to acquire such technologies by theft or bribes and will succeed sooner or later; and that we know from history of charismatic tyrants who rallied throngs of followers, taught them hatred, terrorized whole populations, and exploited a severe national crisis to grab dictatorial power. Instead of integrating these well-known facts to shine a shaft of light on the future, we cling to the conventional wisdom: that democracies will remove these threats from our planet by promoting political freedom, economic growth, and free trade.

But this wisdom will crumble instantly when a nation is attacked from within—suddenly and clandestinely—with a nuclear or advanced biological weapon causing immense damage and casualties. At that moment, the surviving military and civilian leadership in the attacked country, as well as governments of other nations, will find themselves in a world without guideposts. The lessons of military history will be of no avail. Thucydides on the Peloponnesian War, the outpourings of modern think tanks, and everything in between will all be useless in the shattering new situation. Because of the transforming novelty of such an attack, new national security concepts must be developed well before the onslaught occurs. Wide-ranging preparatory measures must be implemented in advance.

Military leaders routinely develop war plans for possible conflicts, particularly those started by an enemy surprise attack. So we should not flinch from planning against annihilation from within. War plans help the armed forces and government leaders to focus on the purpose of fighting the war—to expel an invader, to defeat an aggressor who initiated an all-out war, to occupy an area that needs to be pacified. We need new plans to reflect our utterly new situation.

This is not the first time we have been asked to rethink our strategies in the wake of a transformed political and technological environment. Following the first use of nuclear weapons in 1945, American and British statesmen sensed instantly that entirely new strategic goals would be needed. Within a few years, nuclear deterrence and non-proliferation became the key strategic objectives of the nuclear age. As indicated earlier (in chapter 3), both were only partially successful. We have seen that nuclear deterrence as a strategy for preventing attacks with *conventional* arms was oversold, while the policies against proliferation were gradually undone by the curse of "dual use." In any event, the grand strategy of the nuclear age—deterrence combined with non-proliferation—will not offer an adequate conceptual basis for averting annihilation from within. Indeed, it is the inadequacy of non-proliferation policies that requires us to devise a new security concept. And given the mentality and elusive ubiquity of those who might seek to annihilate a nation from within, nuclear deterrence will be of only marginal value.

How should this new challenge be approached? Begin by imagining the needs of the national leadership in the immediate post-attack environment. Decisions with momentous consequences would have to be reached instantly. Special technologies to gather intelligence would have to be ready and in place. Previously enacted standby emergency laws would be essential to manage the aftermath. If we left the planning of all these responses until after the attack, we would obviously be too late. Yet few defense experts have come to grips with this preplanning agenda.

Since the requirements for each nation differ, I shall focus the following discussion mainly on the United States.

The Heart of the Matter

The American defense community has focused creatively on another transformation—the "revolution in military affairs." This transformation is driven by improvements in military technology, such as robots that can search and destroy a target, new intelligence and space capabilities, missiles with pinpoint accuracy, and many more.[1] These innovations are revolutionizing warfare between nations—but annihilation from within is not about wars between nations. It is about a sudden attack using massive violence designed to deprive a nation of its government. For extreme anarchists, the objective of the attack would be to create political chaos, from which, they believe, the ideal political order will emerge. For an aspiring dictator, the objective would be to replace the annihilated government with his own rule.

To thwart unprecedented attacks that could annihilate the United States from within, we must construct a new type of war plan, combined with pre-positioned emergency measures. Let us call the totality of these preparations the Ultimate Emergency Plan. It would complement but not displace current war plans or other preparatory policies. We will still want deterrence to dissuade any nuclear-armed power from launching a nuclear attack against another country—now a remote risk, one hopes. The strategic objectives and military forces that have served us well in hunting down Muslim terrorists might be needed for several decades. Clearly, the United States ought to keep many arrows in the quiver.

The violent and stealthy onslaughts designed to annihilate a nation from within are unique in a way that makes defensive measures and counteroffensives extraordinarily difficult. I shall try to demystify the anatomy of these stealthy onslaughts by providing a brief sketch of their unique factors:

■ First, very few people would be needed to carry out the attack. A single individual could spread a nationwide pandemic using a highly contagious virus. A two-person team would be sufficient to deploy and detonate a couple of nuclear weapons. America's vast intelligence systems focus largely on individual evildoers to track down collaborators, conspirators, and supporters of Al Qaeda or other terrorist organizations. This people-centered approach might easily miss a couple of perpetrators who do their deed alone and know how to avoid telephone calls and other careless ways of revealing themselves. Hence, intelligence gathering needs to be complemented with effective technologies that can detect a nuclear weapon before it is delivered to its target.

■ Second, our enemies may acquire weapons of mass destruction via procedures for which we have no ready response. Although nuclear weapons will be more difficult to acquire than biological ones, it cannot be ruled out that an anarchist cult might motivate a couple of nuclear scientists to build a relatively low-yield nuclear bomb with stolen high-enriched uranium. In 1966 nuclear physicist Theodore Taylor wrote (in the memorandum cited in the previous chapter): "The knowledge necessary for the construction of transportable fission explosives is rapidly becoming understood by increasing numbers of people all over the world." Forty years later, this danger surely has not gone away.

■ Third, if the attack has been properly planned and carried out, the U.S. Government may not know for some time who caused it. The intelligence services will presumably be unable to identify either the individuals who deployed the weapon, or the organization—if any—that supported them, or the foreign sources that may have supplied the weapon, knowingly or otherwise. These massive uncertainties could wreak political havoc.

■ Fourth, the very nature of the attack, and the possibility of follow-on attacks, will demand instant responses by the surviving government officials. The legitimacy of our post-attack government will be at stake in this response, since signs of uncertainty could trigger a downward spiral of political disintegration.

- Fifth on this list is a wild card. There is no law of physics requiring that weapons of mass destruction be nuclear, or chemical, or biological. In the coming decades, other technologies will be developed or rediscovered that can be misused to cause novel types of mass destruction.

These are some of the problems the Ultimate Emergency Plan has to address. Providing a full description of the Plan with all its component measures would take me way beyond the scope of this book. But several specific examples will illustrate the kinds of measures needing to be tackled now.

1. DETECTING NUCLEAR BOMBS Those who attempt to annihilate a nation from within by employing a few nuclear bombs must ensure that their bombs remain concealed until they have been detonated. This obvious fact holds true whether the bombs have been acquired abroad by a tyrant planning a power grab, smuggled into the country by one of the contemporary terrorist organizations, or manufactured at home by an anarchist cult like Aum Shinrikyo, which made its poison gas within earshot of the Japanese police. A top priority for the Ultimate Emergency Plan is the development of sensors and other technologies to detect concealed nuclear bombs.

Against nuclear weapons or fissile material smuggled from abroad, one of our first lines of defense is the Nunn-Lugar program for safeguarding the Soviet nuclear detritus (see chapter 3). Another is the multinational Proliferation Security Initiative of the Bush administration, which aims to intercept weapons of mass destruction that are being smuggled on ships. These efforts abroad would benefit greatly from better detection systems; and for the last line of defense at home, powerful new detection technology is essential. Although specific measures to respond to this priority have been recommended repeatedly, their implementation has proceeded at a snail's pace. In 1995 and 1997, the Pentagon's Defense Science Board conducted studies that explained in plain terms the need for better sensor technologies. Dr. Lowell Wood, a brilliant innovator who is a Senior Scientist at Lawrence Livermore National Laboratory, was one of the participating experts and contributed creative ideas for detecting nuclear bombs.[2] As a participant in the 1997 study, I naively expected that a research effort on nuclear sensors would be started forthwith.

During the next five years, essentially nothing was done. In 2002, at last, the Defense Science Board established a new task force that issued the report "Preventing and Defending Against Clandestine Nuclear Attack" (published in 2004 and readable at www.acq.osd.mil/dsb/reports/2004). Dr. Richard Wagner, a senior nuclear scientist with Los Alamos National Laboratory, chaired this task force, of which I was a member. When our report was completed, Wagner and I agreed that now, indeed, it was time to get serious. So we embarked on a campaign to convince appropriate officials throughout the U.S. Government of the urgent need for a project that could give us some real solutions. By "real solutions" we did not mean endless interagency meetings and spiral-bound reports. A cavalcade of reports will not protect the country.[3]

To find the solutions we desperately need, the U.S. Government should have established a generously funded, well-focused national project, run by a highly competent manager who would be given the authority to enlist and empower the best scientists at the national nuclear laboratories and universities. Over the years, successful projects of this kind have included the Manhattan Project and the Apollo Project. Richard Wagner and I were not alone in our self-chosen mission to convince senior U.S. officials of the need for this project. We were joined by Dr. John Foster (former director of Lawrence Livermore National Laboratory), Ambassador David Abshire (a leader of think tanks and advisor to many presidents), Norman Augustine (former chairman of the Lockheed Corporation), and other luminaries. We talked to numerous senior officials, from Vice

President Cheney on down. None of them disagreed with us that it was time for a serious R&D project on nuclear-detection technology. Yet sadly, it took another three years to get a rather dilatory project started.

No single malfeasance in the U.S. Government can be blamed for the delay in starting this project, but weaknesses in leadership and flawed procedures help explain it. The authority to reach a final decision is often diluted within the bureaucracy, especially for new initiatives on which several agencies claim to have a say. "Authority is spread so thinly that no one can say yes and too many people can say no," wrote John Lehman (a member of the 9/11 commission) of America's recent intelligence reorganization. Also, the officials who are nominally in charge often lack the authority—or the courage—to modify wholly inappropriate regulations that harm the national interest. A welter of harmful accounting regulations prevent the Department of Energy from making the most of its jurisdiction over the national laboratories. Newt Gingrich found that the damaging slowdown of Iraq's reconstruction could have been avoided had common sense replaced the impractical accounting regulations, which everyone felt compelled to follow.[4] Another reason for the neglect of nuclear-detection technology by the U.S. Government is the American tradition of defining "national security" and the mission of the Defense Department as the protection of American interests *beyond* the shores, to the exclusion of U.S. territory. As Stephen Flynn points out, America is the only country that "continues to treat domestic and national security as distinguishable from one another."[5]

After interminable interagency meetings, the U.S. Government bureaucracy created the Domestic Nuclear Detection Office, located in the Department of Homeland Security. Or more accurately, it created a large organization-chart for a new office meant to design and manage the overall architecture of detecting and interdicting smuggled nuclear weapons. But to design an "architecture" for detecting smuggled nuclear weapons without knowing more about the detection technology is like designing a nation's air force, with all its bases, personnel, and logistics, without knowledge about the aircraft that will be built. A vigorous R&D project on this technology ought to be the first priority, since it will take years to invent and develop effective technology and to produce prototypes.

Curiously, midlevel bureaucrats repeatedly opposed such an R&D project, pretending "the limits of physics" would preclude significant progress in detection technology. In fact, it was not the "limits of physics" but the bureaucrats' limited knowledge of physics that blocked progress. Senior officials in the Defense Department knew better. They recognized the importance of developing more effective means against smuggled nuclear weapons. Secretary Rumsfeld approved a new Quadrennial Defense Review in February 2006, and this guidance for the Pentagon's priorities leaves no doubt about the requirement to detect and render safe nuclear materials and devices.[6] Douglas J. Feith (Undersecretary of Defense for Policy 2001–2005), by ensuring that this requirement became part of the new guidance, changed the Pentagon's role from a bystander to an active participant in the development of such nuclear detection systems. And Ryan Henry (Principal Deputy of the Undersecretary for Policy) skillfully advanced the implementation of the guidance. The Pentagon would be able to move ahead rapidly since its Defense Threat Reduction Agency has the requisite technical and administrative capabilities. Thanks to its highly competent leaders—Dr. James A. Tegnelia and Dr. G. Peter Nanos—the agency could launch an effective integrated project. Yet, as of this writing, obstructionist bureaucrats might yet prevail over those of us who reject the idea that America must remain naked to an enemy attack with smuggled nuclear weapons.

2. ASSURING THE CONTINUITY OF THE U.S. GOVERNMENT To eliminate the incumbent government is the central purpose of those who seek to annihilate a nation from within. An aspiring dictator planning a nuclear power-grab will target the political leadership. So might anarchists who want to substitute their fantasized nirvana for the legitimate government. Jihadists living in Denmark, Belgium, the Netherlands, and other European democracies have already used murder and threats of murder to remove or intimidate parliamentarians and critics of their "faith-based" terrorism.

As noted in the previous chapter, it would be much easier for jihadists to mount a successful nuclear power-grab in one of the authoritarian Central Asian Republics than in an established democracy. But in one respect democracies are peculiarly vulnerable: Unlike dictatorships, they must concern themselves with the constitutional and legal requirements for replacing killed parliamentarians or government officials. During the Cold War, the U.S. Congress and the Executive branch paid considerable attention to the possibility of a Soviet nuclear attack that might devastate Washington. To protect the members of Congress, the second Eisenhower administration built a massive underground bunker, hidden below the fashionable Greenbrier hotel in West Virginia and equipped with communications, assembly rooms, and many other necessities. The whole installation, tucked away under this huge building, remained secret—at least to the public—for thirty years. It is now open to tourists, a sight to be seen. And for visitors with some imagination as to what the installation was all about, the sight is both impressive and deeply depressing. It also attests to the seriousness with which President Eisenhower sought to assure the continuity of Congress despite the worst manmade catastrophe then imaginable. But even the Greenbrier plan had its weaknesses. Like most Cold War measures for the continuity of government, it was predicated on the assumption of several hours' advance warning; and secrecy was also essential.

A properly organized nuclear power-grab would not provide warning, and one nuclear weapon with a yield of those used in 1945 could kill nearly everyone in the U.S. Capitol building from a van parked well beyond the normal security perimeter. While senators killed by such a sneak attack could soon be replaced in most states by the governors, members of the House of Representatives would have to be replaced through special elections in their districts—a slow process even in normal times, and likely to be far slower during what would be the greatest crisis in the nation's history. There are several different ways in which the House might be reconstituted, but it is important to settle on one of them in advance of the crisis. Members of Congress and various commissions have proposed solutions; and Norman J. Ornstein, Resident Scholar at the American Enterprise Institute, has made a strong case for the House itself to take action.[7] Yet the House has thus far failed to agree on an effective solution. In the late 1950s, the U.S. Government had the iron discipline and determination to complete the expensive Greenbrier project. Today, despite the experience of 9/11, Congress cannot even agree on passing a cost-free bill to ensure that a House of Representatives will exist after a super-9/11.

And the issue of the federal government's continuity is not confined to Congress. Consider the replacement of senior officials in U.S. Government agencies and departments. Before being appointed by the President, all prospective senior officials must fill out questionnaires to obtain White House clearance—a process that can be time-consuming, infuriating, and insulting. Did you pay the Social Security taxes for the boy who mows your lawn? Will you divest yourself of all assets that could be construed as a conflict of interest? When the White House apparatchiks are finally satisfied with the answers, the nominee must repeat the whole process to be confirmed by the Senate, instead of being allowed to simply provide a copy of the questions already answered. The nominee has to fill out dozens of additional questionnaires targeting the same issues, but—as if meant to double the workload—using different formats.

How will the President replace cabinet members and other senior officials the morning after an anthrax attack or nuclear bomb has killed half the senior officials in Washington? Unless that question has been answered in advance, the President will confront a disastrous dilemma: either wait months until all the forms have been filled out, reviewed, and the confirmation hearings completed; or, more likely, make "interim" appointments, whether legal or not, and navigate with a substitute "cabinet" that lacks constitutional and political approval at precisely the time when the government's legitimacy and legal continuity are of transcendent importance. This is not a problem that requires a study; it has been studied, and it cries for implementation.[8] A tiny drop of foresight and a flyspeck of courage in Congress would solve it.

3. MOBILIZATION LAWS Established democracies generally have laws empowering the president (or prime minister) to restore law and order and strengthen the country's security in the event of an insurrection or armed attack. The U.S. president has several options for dealing with national emergencies. And as Paul Schott Stevens has explained, the legal restrictions on the President's use of military forces in domestic emergencies have frequently been exaggerated, sometimes deliberately by defense officials, in order to prevent military forces being diverted from overseas missions.[9] But what would really be needed in this unique emergency is something akin to a Declaration of War. As envisaged in the Constitution, only Congress can declare war. Last used in World War II, the old-fashioned Declaration of War is far more powerful and comprehensive than any of the President's current emergency authorities. It automatically triggers a host of provisions in the U.S. legal code to support the armed services and provide for industrial mobilization. As part of the Ultimate Emergency Plan that I am suggesting here, a carefully prepared, new presidential emergency declaration could incorporate some of the still useful legal ramifications of the Declaration of War. Of course, the President's authority to issue such an expanded Declaration would have to be legislated by Congress in advance of any mass destruction attack. And when issued it ought to require congressional approval as soon as Congress could function again. But having such a law ready would be of enormous help in managing the extreme crisis.

Indeed, the existence of some such presidential authority might help deter the attack. It is important that anarchists and terrorists be told in advance they cannot annihilate America with a nuclear or biological attack. They might, to be sure, inflict horrifying destruction, casualties, and pain. But if the President (or his successor) is empowered to instantly marshal all of America's strength based on a firm constitutional and legal foundation, the attack would be unlikely to attain its objectives. The final outcome would more likely include the extermination of the individuals who employed the mass destruction weapon, together with all their instigators, financiers, and supporting arms peddlers.

Many thoughtful people are concerned that increased government powers in an emergency will undermine civil liberties, privacy, and human rights. Michael Ignatieff's recent book *The Lesser Evil: Political Ethics in the Age of Terror* has a great deal to contribute on this important problem. It sets forth a nuanced agenda for combining an aggressive war against terrorism with maintenance of democratic institutions. Emergency powers should be carefully designed to preserve essential rights wherever possible and to ensure the restoration of rights when the threat has receded. In the situation where mass destruction weapons have already been used, or are about to be used, most people would want the government to have all the intrusive and "oppressive" powers needed to protect the democratic nation from being destroyed. Which makes it all the more important that legislators draft, and upon careful review adopt, emergency powers beforehand. After the cataclysm, it would be impossible to create the delicate balance between what's immediately needed for survival and what's desirable for the democratic future. A news leak in December 2005 about warrantless wiretaps of U.S. citizens has led to a flood of criticism in the media and angry debate in Congress. That's how democracy must work. But a calamity far worse than 9/11 (which was the event that led to these wiretaps) might strike Washington, and it would behoove Congress—after all its backward-looking debate about warrantless wiretaps—to turn around and look ahead.

The new emergency declaration should also include provisions for industrial mobilization. Administrative preparations by the Roosevelt administration in 1940–41 helped greatly in accomplishing America's enormous mobilization after the Pearl Harbor attack. In August 1941, President Roosevelt established the Supply, Priorities, and Allocation Board, charged with dividing available materials among military and civilian needs. After December 7, 1941, the automotive industry rapidly shifted its plants and labor force to the production of tanks.[10] For the kind of attack considered here, the standby authorities for industrial mobilization would obviously not be about tanks, but about technologies for use against weapons of mass destruction—from vaccines to nuclear sensors. Assume, for instance, that prior to a stealthy use of a nuclear bomb, highly effective nuclear-detection technology had been developed but not yet mass-produced and deployed. At that point, the mobilization authority would empower the government rapidly to move from the production of consumer goods all the materials, plants, and workforce needed to produce thousands of these sensors.

4. GUARDING TERRITORIAL SOVEREIGNTY In times of domestic upheaval as well as in wars between nations, a country's sovereign territory is the decisive arena. The military strategist Colin S. Gray puts it well: "The modern state is legally a territorial entity, and nearly everything that we care about deeply exists on land. . . . Human beings do not live at sea, or in cyberspace."[11] After an attack from within employing mass destruction weapons, the nation's sovereign territory would be a contested arena. Unfortunately, democracies have become increasingly beholden to deeply flawed policies and various United Nation conventions that limit their ability to govern their sovereign territory.

The underlying facts of this predicament are well known, but their interpretation is a controversial topic. It triggers bitter clashes of conflicting ethical principles and disputes about multiculturalism, open borders, xenophobia and xenophilia, the merits of international law, and other hot-button issues.

The UN Asylum Convention affords a spectacular example of the new restrictions on countries' control of their territory. The right of asylum has become an ethical imperative so compelling as to forestall discussion of its associated absurdities. Does flight from political repression qualify anyone for asylum? In principle, it should, according to the original concept of asylum. But in practice that is wholly impossible, since three billion people on this planet live under political repression. So the contrived limitation of the Asylum Convention is that the applicant must have managed to put a foot across the border of a host country. At that point, the host country's asylum bureaucracy and international monitors take over, endlessly blocking any effort to weed out fraudulent claimants. In the United States and in Western Europe political elites with blinkered conscience defend the system because they can calmly ignore the three billion people living under repressive despots. These masses of people—oh, how convenient—are unable to meet the condition for claiming asylum, namely to cross the border of a magnanimous democracy.

But there have been occasions in which asylum seekers approach the territory of the wealthy democracies not just in small groups, but as rippling waves that look like harbingers of an immense flood tide. Instantly, the democracies on which these harbingers intrude become fearful and try to revise their asylum laws. Yet the UN asylum police and holier-than-thou legislators won't allow this. Unable to change the law, the executive branches of the affected governments feel compelled to cheat audaciously. In 1992–93, throngs of Haitians sought to escape their nation's turmoil and poverty by reaching American territory on any available vessel. The Clinton administration's response was to intercept the ships fleeing from Haiti and to bribe the Haitian government to let the U.S. Coast Guard escort them back home before the would-be refugees could land and claim asylum under the UN Asylum Convention.[12] Nations of the European Union have made similar deals with East European and African countries. When ships with smuggled immigrants from Asia approached American shores, the U.S. Government has intercepted the vessels and pleaded with Mexico, Guatemala, or Honduras to let the Coast Guard escort the ships to their countries where the less fastidious legal practices would sweep all the asylum claims into a wastebasket and allow quick repatriation of the whole human cargo. In 2005 the socialist government of Spain countered the flow of African asylum seekers by surrounding Ceuta and Melilla (the Spanish exclaves in Africa) with double fences, and made a deal with Morocco to take back any would-be asylum seekers who made it over the razor wires atop those fences.

These devious procedures for coping with the UN Asylum Convention unmask the present asylum policies as a hypocritical hoax. People who suffer the worst political repression—say, in North Korea, Burma, or the Darfur region of the Sudan—cannot escape from their prison-like existence; while the present asylum system discriminates in favor of migrants who want to leave their homes for economic reasons and can pay generous bribes to people-smugglers. Surely, this hypocrisy could be replaced by a more honest and more realistic human rights policy.

The origin of today's asylum practices is the United Nations Asylum Convention of 1951. Voting for this UN Convention in 1951 was a gesture of atonement to acknowledge the inherited guilt of having abandoned refugees from Nazi Germany before and during World War II. And it was a painless gesture. The 1951 Convention applied only to people seeking asylum "as a result of events occurring before 1 January 1951." But sixteen years later a Protocol was added to this Convention with staggering consequences. This 1967 Protocol created a vast, open-ended obligation to offer asylum to *future* refugees.[13] It was drafted in the bowels of the United Nations by lawyers specializing in refugee matters and was adopted by the U.S. Congress and most European parliaments with minimal or no debate. A small bureaucratic conclave thus succeeded in changing global immigration policies by stealth, with huge and irreversible consequences for all democracies. The Senate Foreign Relations Committee held its hearing on the Protocol on September 20, 1968. The State Department witness told the senators that the number of asylum seekers from Eastern Europe could not be predicted, yet he totally ignored the predictability of the immensely larger flow from the rest of the world. Sensing a cover-up, Senator John Sparkman, who chaired the hearing, asked the State Department witness: "I want to make certain of this: Is it absolutely clear that nothing in this protocol . . . requires the United States to admit new categories or numbers of aliens?" The State Department witness answered: "That is absolutely clear"—an answer that turned out to be absolutely wrong. Such utterly wrong forecasts have been all too common when the U.S. administration urged Congress to adopt a new immigration law.

More serious is the well-established fact that the current asylum procedures undermine the security of democracies. It has been amply documented in news reports and by government commissions that dozens of terrorists who participated in the attacks in Europe and the United States—before 9/11, during 9/11, and since then—have been able to do so by taking advantage of the flawed asylum system. The fatuity of it all has no limits. Recall that after 9/11, British and Dutch soldiers fought in Afghanistan with their American allies to root out the cruelly oppressive Taliban regime. Yet a couple of years later, a Taliban soldier who had *fought against* the British liberators fled from the new Afghanistan and was granted asylum in England. He was not the only Taliban whose asylum claim was being processed by the British authorities. Why grant them asylum? Incredibly, the rationale was that they feared persecution by the new, democratic Afghan authorities. In addition, more than two thousand asylum applicants from Afghanistan reached the Netherlands in 2003 and 2004. In accordance with the UN Asylum Convention, they had to be processed, and after years of protracted legal wrangling the chances were good for hundreds of them to remain in the Netherlands. Since NATO forces had liberated Afghanistan by that time and worked to restore democracy, one wonders how many of these applicants were Taliban soldiers or sympathizers, that is to say, not the politically oppressed but the oppressors.[14] Would England or the Netherlands in 1947 have granted asylum to members of the Waffen-SS who feared persecution by the new, democratic government in Bonn? As the scolds in ancient Greece and Rome used to say: *quod Deus perdere vult, dementat prius* (whom God wants to destroy, He first disables with stupidity).

5. NATIONAL UNITY Of all the ingredients needed to defeat an attempted annihilation from within, perhaps the most important is national unity. This holds true for the United States, England, Japan, Germany, France, indeed for any democracy that might be attacked. A shining example for all was the Churchill-Attlee government created in May 1940. Following the German invasion of Holland and Belgium, Prime Minister Neville Chamberlain realized that he ought to step down, and Churchill was called to form a new government—the National Coalition Government. At first, Churchill came under considerable pressure to purge ministers who had been responsible for the Munich agreement with Hitler and for Britain's inadequate war preparations. But he would not join "the would-be heresy-hunters." As he explains in his memoirs: "Official responsibility rested upon the Government of the time. But moral responsibilities were more widely spread. . . . No one had more right than I to pass a sponge across the past." Throughout the war, Attlee and his Labor Party loyally supported the National Coalition Government. "It was a proud thought," Churchill recalls, "that the Parliamentary Democracy . . . can endure, surmount, and survive all trials. Even the threat of annihilation did not daunt our Members, but this fortunately did not pass."[15]

David Reynolds, in his masterful and probing study of Churchill's memoirs of the Second World War, adds a thought-provoking enrichment to Churchill's own account of his struggles to maintain national unity and also lead the nation's fight for survival. "Both struggles absorbed a huge amount of time and emotional energy. Churchill recognized the bleakness of Britain's predicament—whatever his public bravado, there were moments of private doubt—and he had to adduce plausible reasons for fighting on. . . . To see the whole picture makes Churchill a more impressive figure than the almost blindly pugnacious bulldog of popular stereotype."[16]

It is an edifying story to this day. National unity was essential for that success. It was also essential for the United States—during the war as well as afterward, when the time came to establish democracy in Japan and Germany. Thanks to Franklin Roosevelt's and Harry Truman's ability to maintain bipartisan support on many foreign policy issues, America could play a predominant and constructive role in shaping the new world order. Both presidents enlisted the support of Republican Senator Arthur Vandenberg to prepare the Senate's acceptance of the United Nations, and Truman asked the Republican statesman John Foster Dulles to negotiate the Japanese peace treaty. To end America's isolationism, Roosevelt and Truman had the political sophistication that Woodrow Wilson lacked. Yet many academics describe that successful American engagement in world affairs as "Wilsonian." Given the global havoc that Woodrow Wilson caused, one wonders whether academics revere Wilson merely because he was one of them.

6

RESTORATION

THE HISTORY OF THE HUMAN RACE is a saga with many sad endings. Down through the centuries, a new beginning has followed each demise and new civilizations have been built on the ruins of the old. Whenever a nation or an empire had lost its power, pride, and glory, the waning societies have been replenished by a new influx of people—or alas, have been superseded by multitudes of barbarians. In any event, the decline and fall of great cultures rarely erased the memories of their splendorous past. We still treasure the literature and philosophy of the Roman Empire, long after the sack of Rome in the fifth century and the fall of Constantinople in 1453.

But new Great Destroyers are now arriving on stage—the spread of mass destruction weapons beyond national control, and technologies that can invade the sanctuary of the human mind. These trends will make possible a nuclear power-grab by aspiring tyrants, and in the more distant future might set off an international competition among nations to build a system with superhuman intelligence.

The morning after a nuclear power-grab, fear of follow-on attacks will grip the populace and preoccupy government leaders in many countries. Responding to these deep-felt anxieties, many prominent politicians and academics will clamor for utopian solutions. If biological weapons had been used in the attack, benevolent activists would advocate an international agency to assume worldwide control of all biotechnology laboratories and offer "absolute" assurance that such activities stay within the bounds of peaceful use. If a nuclear bomb had been used for the attack, they would cry out for universal nuclear disarmament. This would be a flashback to the beginning of the nuclear age, when quite a few Americans favored some form of world government to avert nuclear war. The United World Federalists, an organization that attracted politically active and influential Americans in the late 1940s, called for a global federation of nation-states to control nuclear technology, essentially a greatly strengthened United Nations.[1] Even today, proposals for abolishing all nuclear weapons easily gain support. In the fall of 2005, 74 percent of the American public (according to a Pew Research Center poll) favored the United States' signing a treaty to reduce and eventually eliminate all nuclear weapons. The governments struggling to put an end to nuclear or biological stealth attacks must not be distracted by such delusory solutions. Undoubtedly, the advocates of these global agreements will mean well and will bristle with their sense of rectitude.

How on earth could an international treaty prevent another sneak attack with mass destruction weapons—and especially one launched from within a nation? After the first nation was attacked from within, surely every other national government would do its utmost to avert the same fate. How could the United Nations enforce arms control measures that these very same nations could not enforce within their own territory? Would the UN suddenly become a world government with superior enforcement power in every country? And if this magically happened, would we not end up with a world tyranny? As the renowned political theorist Hedley Bull wrote several years ago: "The advocate of world government makes the tacit assumption that it is his own moral and political preferences that will be embodied in it; he conceives the world authority as a projection of his own ideas. . . . One of the difficulties in all prescriptions about future world order is to determine to whom they are addressed. . . . Mankind as such is not a political agent or actor."[2]

Since these proposals for a benignant world authority would woefully fail—save for garnering a couple of Nobel Peace Prizes—we need an alternative. After a clandestine mass destruction attack, the leading nations must first restore their own security before they can commit themselves to join international efforts for controlling destructive technologies. Until the calamity's initial aftermath can be assessed, the multiple pathways for long-term restoration will remain obscured by vast uncertainties. At most, four broad priorities might be anticipated:

- First, for the survival of democracies, their legal and constitutional foundation must be reinstated (or if left undestroyed, must be revitalized). Only if the vast majority of the people regards the government as legitimate can the restoration proceed. The chronic violence and lawlessness in Iraq after 2004 illustrate how a society can become entrapped in a vortex of anarchy.

- Second, the initial period of restoration must somehow find a way back to nuclear nonuse as a lasting dispensation in which national leaders and the public can have some confidence. Obviously, after a nuclear power-grab, there will be lingering uncertainty about nuclear weapons being used again. It will be absolutely essential to prevent this uncertainty from stoking a multipolar nuclear arms race that might end in a nuclear 1914.

- Third, the restoration must focus hard on the global economy. A clandestine use of mass destruction weapons by unknown evildoers will make governments suspect that a foreign terrorist organization might be responsible. The stronger the belief that the deadly weapons were smuggled across the border—even if in fact they originated within the attacked country—the greater will be the pressure to close all borders. If several large trading nations felt obliged to do this, the global economy would collapse, and there would be severe food shortages in several countries.

- Fourth, the spiritual dimension of the restoration will be of great importance. The calamity and suddenness of the annihilating attack will induce people to seek refuge and comfort in transcendental spheres of thought. For many people, the motivating emotions and intellectual imagery will now be about life after death, rewards in paradise, a coming judgment day. One might reasonably regard this change in thinking as beneficial and appropriate for such dreadful times, except that it would make the worldwide clash of religions more violent. Jihadist suicide bombers who are about to kill themselves—the better to kill children or elderly shoppers—are fixated on their promised reward in paradise.

Note also that technology's threat to nation-states derives not just from weapons of mass destruction. The ongoing progress in computer science and brain science will lead to proposals for building a system with superhuman intelligence. Any nation that can command science to work on such a project is likely to pursue it—up to the point where moral scruples call for a halt. But as soon as a major power appears to make significant advances in this area, other nations will wake up to the immense national security implications of superhuman intelligence. As day follows night, they will enter the race with competing projects. Thus, the ultimate threat to nations approaches from two sides. First, if the quest for superhuman intelligence succeeds with a dramatic breakthrough, the identity of the human race will be challenged, as adumbrated in Aldous Huxley's *Brave*

New World. Second, as weapons of mass destruction truly move beyond the control of nation-states, we, or our descendants, may have to cope with the most violent global anarchy.

A frightful question would then grip our mind: have we reached the twilight of the glorious era when technology kept making us ever more prosperous and more comfortable? This era was ushered in by mankind's cultural split more than two centuries ago, and led to a widening divergence between the scientific mode of human activity and the societal-political mode. Must this divergence end in the destruction of the world's entire political and social matrix? How can nation-states—indeed, how can the human race—survive scientific-technological advances that keep accelerating, untamed by religion and time-tested traditions and moving way beyond the control of governments? This question will have no easy answer. Nations now depend on perpetual economic growth, which thrives best if nourished with untrammeled technological progress. Perpetual growth of the national economy has many influential advocates, such as the business community, investors, and agencies that seek to reduce poverty. The options of elected officials to tame the dark side of technology are therefore severely limited, since almost any restriction imposed on technological "progress" will be attacked as being antigrowth.

Today's apotheosis of economic growth is a relatively recent phenomenon.[3] It began when Franklin D. Roosevelt energized U.S. and British officials to prepare postwar policies for promoting economic growth at home and abroad, a new philosophy heralded by FDR's famous call for "freedom from want—everywhere in the world." Prior to the 1930s' Great Depression, many industrializing nations had enjoyed fairly steady growth for a long time without any specific pro-growth policies and without pro-growth lobbies. Yet today, being considered "pro-growth" is essential for politicians seeking reelection and for economists seeking an academic career. Few scholars are willing to explore the merits and problems of what John Stuart Mill called the "stationary state"—an economic-demographic order in which human lives could continue being enriched and people would make cultural advances, although the world's population and "physical capital" would have stabilized. Someone who has written creatively on the larger picture of growth and stability is Herman E. Daly; but economists who see merit in some such stability are not welcome in the economics departments of most universities.[4] That leaves us intellectually ill-prepared to throttle the dark side of technology without stumbling into a prolonged economic depression.

To find our way through these times of trouble we will have to reject the siren songs of new ideologies that promise security for everyone, but at the price of accepting a totalitarian dictatorship. How can democratic nations rein in science and technology to work again as their servants, not as their destroyers? How can a people find the strength and conviction to turn around the flow of history?

In meeting this formidable challenge, an important source of strength can be the people's common emotional bond with the past. In the United States, this bond is the extraordinary continuity of the American Constitution. No other global power has been built on such an enduring foundation, providing both a long-lasting political philosophy and extraordinarily stable legal basis for the nation. Certainly the Roman Empire changed its legal structure and political philosophy several times, as did the British Empire, and China had its dynastic changes as well as the more recent revolutionary transformations of its ideology. But the American Constitution is truly exceptional. While it has been amended many times and disputes about its interpretation enliven America's political scene endlessly, let us note that no American party, no organization with any influence, none of America's ethnic and racial groups oppose the Constitution. To preserve this most precious patrimony of our country, each generation must be reminded of the gift from the Founding Fathers. We all must maintain the emotional link to the time of the country's creation, even as we also must look to the future—both its promising prospects and ominous threats.

Fortunately, the human mind can rise above the inexorable flow of time. As if lifted up by celestial wings, our emotions enable our thoughts to overcome the transitory nature of the current moment. We can revisit moods of erstwhile happiness or sorrow, and leap ahead in joyous expectation or with grim foreboding. These winged emotions revive the vanished past to provide an anchor for our present sentiments, and illuminate a future that is still out of reach. What binds people together in times of trouble are emotional links to stories of their past endeavors, their sacrifices and victories, their wellsprings of ethics and faith. What inspires people to accept sacrifice today to build a better tomorrow are the colors of hope and fear that illuminate the road ahead. Without these emotive anticipations and memories, societies would live compressed in the here and now. Perched on such a narrow foothold in the time dimension, people would lack the inspiration—indeed, would lack the will—to exert themselves in behalf of the future.

NOTES

1. Mankind's Cultural Split

The epigraph lines at the beginning of this chapter from Johann Wolfgang von Goethe's *Faust* (*Zwei Seelen wohnen, ach! In meiner Brust, die eine will sich von der andern trennen;* . . .) are followed by a passage suggesting that the "two souls" represent the struggle between the desire for earthly pleasures and a striving for higher values. Although this is not exactly my theme in the present chapter, the central theme of the Faust legend—as developed by Goethe, Christopher Marlowe, and other authors—is highly relevant to this book. Significantly, this legend gained popularity at the dawn of the scientific-industrial revolution. The legend speaks to man's pursuit of ever more scientific knowledge that will bring ever more power over nature and with it more material pleasures, even at the risk of causing fatal damage to one's traditional moral values—a gamble known as the Faustian bargain with the devil.

1. Jon Turney's *Frankenstein's Footsteps: Science, Genetics, and Popular Culture* (New Haven: Yale University Press, 1998) offers an engrossing account of the literary premonitions that preceded Mary Shelley's book, and the sequel of science and science fiction since then. Turney notes that Mary Shelley "belonged to a society seeing the first real effects of industrialization, when whole landscapes marked by

'dark satanic mills' were becoming visible. And she was witness to the growing power of science" (19).

2. A recent book on China's short-lived naval triumph is Louise Levathes, *When China Ruled the Seas:The Treasure Fleet of the Dragon Throne, 1405–1433* (New York: Oxford University Press, 1996). My quote above of Wen-yuan Qian is from his *The Great Inertia: Scientific Stagnation in Traditional China* (London: Croom Helm, 1985), 106; and of Donald J. Munro from his *The Imperial Style of Inquiry in Twentieth Century China* (Ann Arbor: University of Michigan, Center for Chinese Studies, 1996), 7–8. Joseph Needham's *The Grand Titration: Science and Society in East and West* (London: Allen & Unwin, 1969), although based on his magistral study of early Chinese discoveries and inventions, fails to reach a convincing answer to "the fundamental question" (finally posed on page 150!): "why did modern science not arise in China?"

3. According to Paul Mantoux, "science came later [in the emergence of the Industrial Revolution] and brought its immense reserves of power to bear on the development which had already begun, thus giving at once to partial developments in different industries a common direction and a common speed." Mantoux, *The Industrial Revolution in the Eighteenth Century* (New York: Harper & Row, 1961; original French edition in 1906), 475.

Joel Mokyr observes that "the fruits of the Industrial Revolution were slow in coming. Per capita consumption and living standards increased little initially, but production technologies changed dramatically" (*The Lever of Riches: Technological Creativity and Economic Progress* [New York: Oxford University Press: 1990], 83). Mokyr also notes that after 1850, "science became more important as a handmaiden of technology" (113.)

Many scholars have offered explanations for the intriguing question of why industrialization and modern science first arose in Western Europe. For a richly documented overview, see Jack A. Goldstone, "The Rise of the West—or Not? A Revision of Socio-economic History," *Sociological Theory* (July 2000): 175–94.

4. I am in agreement here with Samuel P. Huntington's list of characteristics of "Western" society: the classical legacy, Catholicism and Protestantism, European languages, separation of church and state, social pluralism, representative government bodies, and individualism; but not science and technology. Huntington, *The Clash of Civilizations and the Remaking of World Order* (New York; Simon & Schuster: 1996), 69–72.

The contrary argument—that modern science and "Western" culture are organically linked—has been advanced both by scholars who are optimistic about the future of "the West" and by those who dwell on its decline. In his famous *The Decline of the West*, Oswald Spengler maintained that the concept of numbers is culturally conditioned: "eine Zahl an sich gibt es nicht" (*Der Untergang des Abendlandes*, 23d ed., Munich, 1920), 85. Arthur Herman in his book *The Idea of Decline in Western History* (New York: Free Press, 1997) discusses several connections between declinist interpretations of Western culture and an interpretation of modern science and technology as something specifically lodged within Western culture (228–29, 401–402). The optimistic view of the linkage between Western values and modern science is alluded to in Francis Fukuyama, *The End of History and the Last Man* (New York: Free Press, 1992)—for example, his observation that "scientific inquiry proceeds best in an atmosphere of freedom" (93).

5. Fernand Braudel, *A History of Civilizations*, first published in 1963 in France as *Le Monde actuel, histoire et civilizations*, here quoted from Richard Mayne's translation (New York: Penguin Books, 1995), 9. As Braudel points out, the noun *culture* has been appropriated by anthropologists to denote primitive societies in contrast to the "civilizations" of more developed societies. But he adds that "the useful adjective 'cultural,' invented in Germany about 1850, suffers from none of these complications. It applies, in fact, to the *whole* of the content of a civilization or a culture" (9).

6. Zbigniew Brzezinski, *Between Two Ages: America's Role in the Technetronic Era* (New York: Viking, 1970), 52. Perhaps the best known of Jacques Ellul's many writings is *The Technological Society* (New York: Knopf, 1970); first published in 1964 as *La Technique: L'enjeu du siècle*.

Some readers might recall C. P. Snow's lecture *The Two Cultures and a Second Look* (Cambridge: Cambridge University Press, 1964), and because of the title might assume that it is related to this chapter. It is totally unrelated. The gravamen of Snow's lecture is that those Western "intellectuals" who are interested in literature, history, and art fail to learn anything about hard science.

7. The distinguishing characteristics of a nation are not self-evident. A sophisticated exploration of the meanings of *nation* and *nationalism* is Benedict Anderson, *Imagined Communities: Reflections on the Origin and Spread of Nationalism* (London: Verso, 1991). Other important contributions are Elie Kedourie, *Nationalism* (Oxford: Blackwell, 1960); Ernest Gellner, *Nations and Nationalism* (Oxford:

Blackwell, 1983); and E. J. Hobsbawm, *Nations and Nationalism Since 1780* (Cambridge: Cambridge University Press, 1990).

8. *The Tyranny of Distance: How Distance Shaped Australia's History* is the title of Geoffrey Blainey's book about the history of Australia (Melbourne: Macmillian, 1975). The evolution of Australia's society, culture, and economy illustrates dramatically the transforming impact of technological advances in the means of transportation.

    The Battle of New Orleans, actually a series of battles ending on January 8, 1815, was fought between British and American soldiers with the commanders on both sides unaware that a peace treaty had been signed in Ghent two weeks earlier.

9. On the coordination of an international telegraph system, see Daniel R. Headrick, *The Invisible Weapon: Telecommunications and International Politics, 1851–1945* (New York: Oxford University Press, 1991), 13. On the synchronization of time zones, see Stephen Kern, *The Culture of Time and Space, 1880–1918* (Cambridge: Harvard University Press, 1983), 12–13.

10. John Gray, *Al Qaeda and What it Means to Be Modern* (London: Faber & Faber, 2003), 110.

2. Science Pushes Us Over the Brink

1. Letter of John Paul II to the Elderly (1999), §9. It is difficult to arrive at a practical definition of natural death. See Stuart J. Younger, Robert M. Arnold, and Renie Shapiro, eds., *The Definition of Death: Contemporary Controversies* (Baltimore: Johns Hopkins University Press, 1999). Various experiments have been reported where scientists tried to keep an animal's head alive by substituting artificial devices for the heart or lungs (24–25). Had these experiments kept the head alive indefinitely, would veterinary science have made the animal immortal?

2. The beliefs regarding mortality vary among different faiths. The ancient Greeks and Romans understood immortality as a privilege reserved for gods. In Christianity, Islam, and other religions, human mortality is foreordained, and the vision of "eternal life" refers to a transcendental existence, a state of being *after* death that lies beyond the earthly matrix of time and space. This transcendental life-after-death is seen as a continuation of one's personal identity in Christianity, and (less explicitly) in Judaism. In Asian religions (Buddhism, Hinduism, Confucianism), the final stage after life on Earth is an im-

personal oneness with all beings. How the views and teachings about death by philosophers and religions have changed through the ages is well documented in Jacques Choron, *Death and Western Thought* (New York: Macmillan, 1963).

3. Some minimal adjustments in the retirement age have been found politically acceptable. In the United Sates, the retirement age of 65 will be raised two months per year until 2008, when it will reach 66. In France in 2003, Prime Minister Jean-Pierre Raffarin courageously pressed the parliament to accept legislation raising the retirement age some three years. Yet in regional elections a year later, Raffarin suffered a crushing setback (the voters' revenge for having to work past age 55?).

   A dramatic treatment of the economic implications of aging is Peter G. Peterson, *Gray Dawn: How the Coming Age Wave Will Transform America—and the World* (New York: Times Books, 1999). Ten years earlier Peter G. Peterson had alerted the country to this problem in a book coauthored with Neil Howe, *On Borrowed Time: How the Growth in Entitlement Spending Threatens America's Future* (New York: Simon & Schuster, 1988).

4. That positive consequences can flow from serious social or political crises is a point made by Yehezkel Dror in his study on governance and policymaking: *The Capacity to Govern: A Report to the Club of Rome* (London: Frank Cass, 2002). Yehezkel Dror is professor at Hebrew University (Jerusalem) and has written creatively on policy planning and broad strategic problems.

5. William F. Ogburn, "Cultural Lag as a Theory," *Sociology and Social Research* (January–February 1957): reprinted in Otis Dudley Duncan, *William F. Ogburn on Culture and Social Change* (Chicago: University of Chicago Press, 1977). For legislative remedies from the 1960s and 1970s to mitigate the harmful effects of technology, see Edmond W. Lawless, *Technology and Social Shock* (New Brunswick: Rutgers University Press, 1977).

6. Erik Erikson's theory of psychosocial development distinguishes eight stages, from infancy to late adulthood, according to their emotive tendencies or moods. Erik H. Erikson, *Childhood and Society* (New York: Norton, 2d ed., 1963), 269–74.

7. A broad treatment of the ethical issues of biotechnology innovations, illuminated by a profound understanding of political philosophy, is Francis Fukuyama, *Our Posthuman Future: Consequences of the Biotechnology Revolution* (New York: Farrar, Straus & Giroux, 2002).

8. Mikhail Heller, *Cogs in the Wheel: The Formation of Soviet Man* (New York: Knopf, 1988). The " Soviet man" idea was satirized by Yevgeniy Zamyatin's anti-utopian novel *We* (1924), a precursor of Aldous Huxley's *Brave New World*. In Zamyatin's novel, a surgical intervention in the brain makes the conversion to "Soviet man" irreversible.

9. *Proceedings of the National Academy of Sciences*, online edition, May 30–June 3, 2005.

10. On the genetically induced memory enhancement, see Joe Z. Tsien, "Building a Brainier Mouse," *Scientific American* (April 2000): 62–68. On the learning-related plasticity: Z. Josh Huang et al., "BDNF Regulates the Maturation of Inhibition and the Critical Period of Plasticity in Mouse Visual Cortex," *Cell* 98 (September 17, 1999): 739–55. Although the totality of intelligence appears to be polygenic, the same genetic factors influence different intellectual abilities (Robert Plomin, "Genetics of Childhood Disorders: Genetics and Intelligence," *Journal of the American Academy of Child and Adolescent Psychiatry* 38 [June 1999]: 786–88).

11. Nobel Laureate Joshua Lederberg wrote in 1963 that "it would be incredible if we did not soon have the basis of developmental engineering technique to regulate, for example, the size of the human brain by prenatal and early postnatal intervention" (in Lederberg's chapter in Gordon Wolstenholme, ed., *Man and His Future* [London: J. and A. Churchill, 1963], 266, a Ciba Foundation volume). Forty years later, research on the genetic determination of the human brain size has, of course, shed more light on this question. A gene that helps determine brain size has been discovered from its disrupted form associated with microcephaly. University of Chicago geneticist Bruce T. Lahn decoded the sequence of this gene in apes and humans and identified changes attributable to natural selection. (This and related studies are summarized by Nicholas Wade, "Evolution of Gene Related to Brain's Growth Detailed," *New York Times*, January 14, 2004.)

Some studies suggest that in Albert Einstein's preserved brain the region supporting mathematical and spatial reasoning was unusually large. See Sandra F. Witelson, D. L. Kigar, and T. Harvey, "The Exceptional Brain of Albert Einstein," *Lancet* 353 (1999): 2149. Steven Pinker, professor of cognitive science at MIT, noted in an Op Ed in the *New York Times* (June 24, 1999) that this finding seemed to conform with Einstein's own observations about the workings of mathematical and spatial reasoning. Since then, however, several neurologists have cast doubt on the findings of the *Lancet* article.

Arthur R. Jensen notes that eight MRI studies of children and adults found significant correlations, close to + .40, between IQ and total brain size, after removing variance due to different body size (*The g Factor: The Science of Mental Ability* [Westport, Conn.: Praeger, 1998], 147). However, M. Henneberg ("Evolution of the Brain: Is Bigger Better?" *Clinical and Experimental Pharmacological Physiology* [September 1998]: 745–49) believes that the correlation between brain size and intelligence might be weak.

12. Ray Kurzweil wrote in *The Age of Spiritual Machines: When Computers Exceed Human Intelligence* (New York: Viking, 1999) that electronic and photonic "machines" will, by the end of this century, be more intelligent entities than humans. He also envisages "virtual bodies" that would provide environmental context and "virtual feelings" for these machines. In his most recent book, *The Singularity Is Near: When Humans Transcend Biology* (New York: Viking, 2005), Kurzweil moves further into his computer world and asserts the dispensability of the human body.

A good overview of ongoing scientific research, science-informed speculations, and unscientific science fiction is Joel Garreau, *Radical Evolution: The Promise and Peril of Enhancing our Minds, Our Bodies—And What It Means to Be Human* (Garden City, N.Y.: Doubleday, 2005). Garreau points out, as I do in this chapter, that China might move ahead of the United States in intelligence enhancement (173).

13. Hubert L. Dreyfus is an early critic of the assertion (made by many proponents of Artificial Intelligence) that lifeless computers can reach, or even surpass, all the important qualities of human intelligence: *What Computers Can't Do* (New York: Harper & Row, 1963). Dreyfus has since authored a new edition of this book: *What Computers Still Can't Do* (Cambridge: MIT Press, 1992). Daniel Crevier, *The Tumultuous History of the Search for Artificial Intelligence* (New York: Basic Books, 1994) also deals with the ambitious advocates in this field and the battles with their critiques. Roger Penrose, a renowned mathematical physicist at the University of Oxford, presents a mathematical argumentation why human consciousness lies beyond computational processes (and hence beyond the capabilities of computers): *Shadows of the Mind: A Search for the Missing Science of Consciousness* (New York and Oxford: Oxford University Press, 1994).

Neuroscience and related disciplines continue to expand our understanding of emotions and their relationship to memory. Eric R. Kandel's recent book offers many examples—for instance, on conscious and unconscious processes of emotion and memory which can be related to different parts of the brain. Kandel, *In Search of Memory: The Emergence of a New Science of Mind* (New York: Norton, 2006), 341–50 and passim.

14. The human brain, by formulating new concepts, can begin to understand new subjects and relate them to previous experience. Computers can establish relationships among subjects in an existing archive but are not effective in forming new concepts. I am indebted to Oleg Favorov, a neuroscientist based at the University of North Carolina, for a memorandum on this aspect of concept formation.

   The World Wide Web brings together computer technology and the social (and linguistic) interaction of large numbers of people. It might thus be seen as a step in the direction of a global Superbrain. Tim Berners-Lee, the principal creator of the World Wide Web, writes: "The analogy of a global brain is tempting, because Web and brain both involve huge numbers of elements—neurons and Web pages—and mixture of structure and apparent randomness." Berners-Lee, *Weaving the Web: The Original Design and Ultimate Destiny of the World Wide Web* (New York: HarperCollins, 2000), 204.

15. An overview of some of these projects can be found in the book by cognitive scientist Andy Clark: *Natural-Born Cyborgs: Minds, Technologies, and the Future of Human Intelligence* (New York and Oxford: Oxford University Press, 2003).

   Attempts have also been made with brain-computer links to overcome blindness from damaged retinas. These experiments have so far been unsuccessful. Fred Hapgood, "Computer Vision and the Dream of the Cyborg," *Cerebrum* (Summer, 2004): 19–32.

16. Even those who work creatively in *both* neuroscience and computer science seem hesitant to explore linkages between computers and the human brain, linkages that might achieve a higher level of intelligence by bringing human emotions into the mix. For example, Jeff Hawkins—a successful computer scientist and entrepreneur with a keen interest in neuroscience (he created the Redwood Neuroscience Institute in California)—wrote the engaging book *On Intelligence* (New York: Times Books, 2004). Yet he dwells on the possible dangers of intelligent robots and seeks to calm the unwarranted fears that intelligent *machines* might take over the world. To this end, he assures us that intelligent machines will not have the emotional faculties of humans (213–16). Why keep this barrier between the emotionless machine-intelligence and the emotion-nourished human intelligence?

A wide-ranging treatment of these issues may be found in Gregory Stock, *Redesigning Humans: Choosing Our Genes, Changing our Future* (Boston: Houghton Mifflin, 2003). But when he addresses the potential for a brain-computer relationship that would yield a higher level of intelligence, Gregory Stock also remains focused on individual human beings whose IQ is somehow to be raised by doing something *within* each brain (23–24). Though Stock (correctly in my view) rejects the idea of brain implants for this purpose (21–22 and 218).

17. Michael Pillsbury's magisterial research of China's military doctrine and strategic planning has given him unique insight into the efforts of Chinese scholars to use elaborate quantitative methods for large-scale geopolitical analyses and forecasts. Among Pillsbury's many books on China's military thought, his *China Debates the Future Security Environment* (Washington D.C.: National Defense University Press, 2000) includes a chapter on "Geopolitical Power Calculations" (203–258). These "calculations" were prepared in exercises carried out by different military teams, using computers and human judgment. The undertaking might well be a precursor of the more recent "facility" (mentioned in Chinese journals) that is meant to "integrate" human judgment with advanced computers.

18. Richard Danzig, *Catastrophic Bioterrorism—What Is to Be Done?* (Washington, D.C.: Government Printing Office, 2003): page 9 on genetically engineered agents; page 2 on "reload."

The Washington-based Center for Strategic and International Studies has a Project on Technology Futures and Global Power, Wealth, and Conflict, directed by Anne G. K. Solomon, which published several reports relevant to dual use (e.g., Gerald L. Epstein, *Global Evolution of Dual-Use Biotechnology* [2005]).

A well-researched history of biological weapons and arms control efforts to control them is Jeanne Guillemin, *Biological Weapons: From the Invention of State-Sponsored Programs to Contemporary Bioterrorism* (New York: Columbia University Press, 2005). The author covers pre–World War II programs, changes in U.S. policy, and other important developments. But she exaggerates the role of the pharmaceutical industry in the Bush administration's rejection of the verification Protocol. That Protocol was rejected because it would not have helped verification in those countries that do not feel bound by so-called "legally binding" agreements.

3. Five Lessons of the Nuclear Age

1. Cited by McGeorge Bundy, *Danger and Survival* (New York: Random House, 1988): Acheson on page 141; Atlee on page 154.

   A rich source for the imagery and emotions evoked by nuclear weapons is Spencer R. Weart, *Nuclear Fear: A History of Images* (Cambridge: Harvard University Press, 1988). Weart mentions many of the public and literary responses since the physicist Fredrick Soddy wrote in 1915: "Imagine, if you can, what the present war would be like if such a [nuclear] explosive had actually been discovered." Weart also covers novels and films of the 1950s and other psychological and literary reactions to the Bomb.

2. Paul Boyer, *By the Bomb's Early Light: American Thought and Culture at the Dawn of the Atomic Age* (Chapel Hill: University of North Carolina Press, 1994), 53.

3. U.S. Department of State, Committee on Atomic Energy, *A Report on the International Control of Atomic Energy* (Washington, D.C.: Government Printing Office, 1946), 32. The Acheson-Lilienthal report became the basis for the Baruch Plan, which addressed more explicitly the refractory problem of verification and enforcement and became the definitive U.S. position that Bernard Baruch presented to the United Nations.

4. Historical research based on archival documents, and memoirs that have become available since the end of the Cold War, make it clear that Stalin would never have agreed to the intrusive international controls that the American proposal required; he relied entirely on the Soviet Union's own nuclear weapons program. See David Holloway, *Stalin and the Bomb: The Soviet Union and Atomic Energy, 1939–1956* (New Haven: Yale University Press, 1994); and Bundy, *Danger and Survival*, 179–82.

5. Robert Jervis, *The Meaning of the Nuclear Revolution: Statecraft and the Prospect of Armageddon* (Ithaca: Cornell University Press, 1989), 70.

   Jacob Viner taught economics at the University of Chicago. His article, "The Implications of the Atomic Bomb for International Relations," appeared in the *Proceedings of the American Philosophical Society* (January 1946): 53–58.

   Alfred North Whitehead explained the "fallacy of misplaced concreteness" in *Process and Reality* (New York: Harper, 1929), 11 and 200. Herman E. Daly deserves credit for pointing out how relevant this fallacy is in contemporary academic theorizing.

6. American and Russian research on the Cuban missile crisis, based on newly available documents, reveals how close this crisis came to triggering a massive nuclear war. Ernest R. May and Philip D. Zelikow, *The Kennedy Tapes: Inside the White House During the Cuban Missile Crisis* (Cambridge: Harvard University Press, 1997); and Philip Zelikow, *Essence of Decision* (New York: Longman, 1998).

Keith Payne has written some of the most penetrating assessments of the hazardous reasoning about nuclear deterrence so rampant during the Cold War. One of his recent books is *The Fallacies of Cold War Deterrence and a New Direction* (Lexington: University of Kentucky Press, 2001).

7. My report has been declassified (and can be purchased from the RAND Bookstore): Fred C. Iklé, with Gerald J. Aronson and Albert Madansky, *On the Risk of an Accidental or Unauthorized Nuclear Detonation*, U.S. Air Force Project RAND RM-2251 (Santa Monica: The RAND Corporation, 1958).

Peter Wyden, in a story on "The Chances of Accidental War," *Saturday Evening Post* (June 3, 1961), provides considerable detail on the concerns about an accidental use of nuclear weapons and safety measures taken at that time. He wrote that my investigations in 1957 were "the first systematic thinking" about this problem. The coded locks for nuclear weapons were called "Permissive Action Links" (or PALs) by the Pentagon in order to convey that these devices are meant to make the weapons *useable* when permitted, not just to *lock* them up. The introduction of PALs proceeded slowly until 1961 when the Kennedy administration vigorously emphasized nuclear safety. See Dan Caldwell, "Permissive Action Links," *Survival* (May–June 1987): 224–38.

8. It was Donald Brennan who coined the acronym MAD for the strategy that embraces this thinking: "The concept of mutual assured destruction provides one of the few instances in which the obvious acronym for something yields at once the appropriate description for it; that is, a Mutual Assured Destruction posture as a goal is, almost literally, mad" (*National Review*, June 23, 1972, 689).

While President Nixon and some of his senior advisors, especially Henry Kissinger, recognized that this MAD strategy *inherited from the Johnson administration* was deeply flawed, they felt the United States could not change course, given, on one side, the pressures by arms control advocates and their Congressional supporters, and, on the other side, the exigencies of the Vietnam War (which had also been inherited from the Johnson administration). So in 1972, Nixon and

Brezhnev signed the ABM Treaty prohibiting missile defenses and the U.S. Senate ratified it with only one dissenting vote.

9. During its last two years, the Clinton administration sought to obtain Russia's consent to the deployment of *limited* missile defenses that would preserve the ABM Treaty and the MAD strategy. To this end it transmitted a memo to Moscow that explained Russia need not fear such limited U.S. defenses since the United States would have to assume Russia's missiles "would be launched after tactical warning." Arms control experts expressed dismay that U.S. negotiators would encourage Russia to maintain such a dangerous alert posture, as if it were something beneficial to the stability of deterrence. See Steven Lee Myers and Jane Pevlez, "Documents Detail U.S. Plans to Alter '71 Missile Treaty," *New York Times*, April 28, 2000, A1; also William J. Broad, "U.S.-Russian Talks Revive Old Debates on Nuclear Warnings," *New York Times*, May 1, 2000, A8.

10. Fred Charles Iklé, "Can Deterrence Last Out the Century?" *Foreign Affairs* (January 1973): 267–85.

11. A carefully researched study of accidents and near-accidents regarding nuclear weapons is Scott D. Sagan's *The Limits of Safety: Organizations, Accidents, and Nuclear Weapons* (Princeton: Princeton University Press, 1993). Also, my above-mentioned *Foreign Affairs* article lists several accidents in military command-and-control systems that should give pause to anyone favoring launch-on-warning. Bruce Blair has studied the Russian launch-on-warning policies of the 1990s and has warned about how these might dangerously interact with U.S. practices (*The Logic of Accidental Nuclear War* [Washington, D.C.: Brookings Institution, 1993]).

12. Peter Hannaford describes this briefing session of Governor Reagan in greater detail in his book *The Reagans: A Political Portrait* (New York: Coward-McCann, 1983), 206–207. A photograph in Hannaford's book (160) captures the episode to which I refer here.

A few weeks after this meeting, Reagan (as presidential candidate) visited the underground command center of the North American Defense Command. There he was told the United States could not defend itself against a single Soviet missile that would have been detected on its way to destroy an American city. Martin Anderson, who had accompanied Reagan on this visit, recalls that Reagan reflected on the terrible dilemma a president would face if, for whatever reason, nuclear missiles were fired at the United States. "The only options he would have," Reagan said, "would be to press the button or do nothing. They're both bad. We should have some way of defending ourselves against nuclear missiles." Martin Anderson, *Revolution* (San Diego: Harcourt Brace Jovanovich, 1988), 83.

13. Caspar Weinberger, *Fighting for Peace* (New York: Warner Books, 1990), 341. On Reagan's attitude toward, and understanding of, nuclear weapons, Paul Lettow wrote the well-documented book, *Ronald Reagan and His Quest to Abolish Nuclear Weapons* (New York: Random House, 2004).

14. Bundy, *Danger and Survival*, 151–52. Churchill dissuaded Eisenhower from speaking publicly about a possible nuclear response to new aggression in Korea (244–45 and 271).

The idea of using nuclear weapons *first* to respond to an attack with conventional forces—or rather to deter it— lived on as NATO doctrine till the end of the Cold War. But in fact, NATO's members were so frightened by the enormous risks of this doctrine that they never dared to explore its consequences. Indeed, NATO war games were routinely stopped at the point where the use of nuclear weapons had to be decided. My critique of NATO's first-use doctrine (Fred C. Iklé, "NATO's 'First Nuclear Use': A Deepening Trap?" *Strategic Review* [Winter 1980]: 18–23) has been vindicated by published documents from Warsaw Pact archives that indicate the Pact was better prepared for "first use" than NATO.

George H. Quester's book, *Nuclear First Strike: Consequences of a Broken Taboo* (Baltimore: Johns Hopkins University Press, 2006) explores the many ramifications and possible long-term impact if the dispensation of nuclear non-use suddenly ended.

15. Holloway, *Stalin and the Bomb*, 306, 336–37. Additional Soviet statements and sources can be found in John Lewis Gaddis, *We Now Know: Rethinking Cold War History* (Oxford: Clarendon Press, 1977), 228–30.

16. Peter G. Boyle, ed., *The Churchill-Eisenhower Correspondence, 1953–1955* (Chapel Hill: University of North Carolina Press, 1990), 123–24. Churchill's stroke some nine months before he wrote this passage was far more serious than the public knew. (See David Reynolds, *In Command of History: Churchill Fighting and Writing the Second World War* [London: Penguin Books, 2005], 440–41.)

Churchill had favored direct negotiations with Stalin since 1950. As the renowned historian David Reynolds reveals (*In Command of History*, 436–39), Churchill even adjusted some of the passages in his *Triumph and Tragedy* so as to refer to Stalin and the Soviet Union with words more appropriate for a future negotiating partner. Stalin's death of course convinced him more strongly that the time was ripe for a U.S.-British-Soviet summit.

17. This effort, which became known as the Nunn-Lugar program, has been highly effective despite "waste and fraud" (that familiar downside of large government programs, including those run by the U.S. Government within the United States). On balance, the program is a splendid—and rare—example of members of Congress taking the lead in initiating an essential policy and seeing it through its implementation. Graham Allison, Director of the Belfer Center at Harvard University, has led a series of projects to alert American and Russian officials to the continuing risk of nuclear theft and smuggled nuclear bombs and to promote more effective countermeasures.

In 2004 Graham Allison offered an update of the Nunn-Lugar program (and related efforts), concluding that nuclear materials, and even finished weapons, have not been adequately protected against theft by terrorist organizations (*Nuclear Terrorism: The Ultimate Preventable Catastrophe* [New York: Henry Holt, 2004]). I would agree with Allison's judgment, but note that this serious negligence stretches over many U.S. administrations and that even the U.S. Government found that some of its own plutonium was unaccounted for. The "missing" U.S. plutonium amounts to almost three metric tons, enough to build several hundred atomic weapons of the 1945 design. See Robert L. Rinne, *An Alternative Framework for the Control of Nuclear Materials* (Stanford University, Calif.: Center for International Security and Cooperation, 1999), 3–5.

18. Henry D. Sokolski, *Best of Intentions: America's Campaign Against Strategic Weapons Proliferation* (Westport, Conn.: Praeger, 2001), 30–33 and 36–37. Sokolski is the founder and Executive Director of the Nonproliferation Education Center.

19. Richard L. Garwin and Georges Charpak, *Megawatts and Megatons: The Future of Nuclear Power and Nuclear Weapons* (Chicago: University of Chicago Press, 2001), 343 and 318.

Henry Sokolski, has written extensively on the dangers of the planned global MOX economy (*see* www.npec-web.org).

4. Annihilation from Within

The Nietzsche quotation at the beginning of this chapter is from *Beyond Good and Evil*, part 4, #146 (*Jenseits von Gut und Böse, Viertes Hauptstück*, 146). Nietzsche connects two sentences. The one quoted above ("Und wenn du lange in einen Abgrund blickst, blickt der Abgrund auch in dich hinein"), and preceding it: "He who fights monsters should be on guard lest he becomes a monster himself" ("Wer mit Ungeheuern kämpft mag zusehen, dass er nicht dabei zum Ungeheuer wird")—a theme to which I shall return in the next chapter.

The Unamuno quotation is from *Tragic Sense of Life (Del Sentimiento Tragico De La Vida En Los Hombres Y En Los Pueblos)* (New York: Dover, 1954), 107. The full sentence is: "Always it comes about that the beginning of wisdom is a fear" ("Siempre resulta que el principio de la sabiduria es un temor").

1. Well before 9/11, Tom Clancy and Russell Seitz published "Five Minutes Past Midnight—and Welcome to the Age of Proliferation," *The National Interest* (Winter 1991–92). The post–9/11 anticipations of a terrorist-type attack with mass destruction weapons include Bill Keller, "Nuclear Nightmares," *New York Times Magazine*, May 26, 2002; Fred Hiatt, "Ignoring the Unthinkable," *Washington Post*, March 17, 2003; George F. Will, "Holocaust in a Suitcase," *Washington Post*, August 29, 2004; Nicholas D. Kristof, "The Nuclear Shadow," *New York Times*, August 14, 2004; Steve Coll, "What Bin Laden Sees in Hiroshima," *Washington Post*, February 6, 2005. Scholars and writers in Europe have also contributed thoughtful anticipations of this calamity. A noteable example is Wolfgang Sofsky, "Diktatur der Angst," *Die Welt (Literaturische Welt)*, November 12 2005.

For a comprehensive overview of Western predictions of cataclysmic disasters and decline, see W. Warren Wagar, *Terminal Visions: The Literature of Last Things* (Bloomington: Indiana University Press, 1982). Wagar reviews the vast literature prophesying man-made calamities and nuclear warfare, from the nineteenth century to the 1980s. Still famous today is H. G. Wells's *The World Set Free*, a story about a devastating nuclear war. Wells finished this book before World War I and lived to witness the nuclear attacks in 1945.

I developed the central theme of this chapter eight years ago in my article "The Next Lenin: On the Cusp and Truly Revolutionary Warfare," *The National Interest* (Spring 1997). I am indebted to Owen Harries, then editor of *The National Interest*, for his encouragement to publish such an article, which was rather premature at that time.

2. For the many definitions of "terrorism" that have been proposed, see Paul R. Pillar, *Terrorism and U.S. Foreign Policy* (Washington, D.C.: Brookings Institution Press, 2001), 12–18. Pillar reports that the U.S. Government, for keeping statistics on terrorism, classifies military personnel who are off-duty as "noncombatants" (14). Walter Laqueur, the preeminent scholar on the history and political dynamic of

terrorism, predicted correctly that disputes about a definition of terrorism "will continue for a long time" and "will make no notable contribution towards the understanding of terrorism" (*The Age of Terrorism* [Boston: Little Brown, 1987], 72).

3. Donald H. Rumsfeld in an editorial in the *Washington Post*, October 26, 2003, B7; President Bush in his speech at Quantico (Virginia), July 11, 2005.

4. Theodore B. Taylor's ideas gained wider attention thanks to the book-length story by *New Yorker* writer John McPhee: *The Curve of Binding Energy: A Journey into the Awesome and Alarming World of Theodore B. Taylor* (New York: Farrar, Straus, and Giroux, 1973). The authors of *America's Achilles' Heel* offer a wealth of information on reports from the last few decades about all kinds of evildoers who used, or tried to use, biological agents, chemical poisons, and sham nuclear bombs (Richard A. Falkenrath, Robert D. Newman, and Bradley A. Thayer, *America's Achilles' Heel* [Cambridge: MIT Press, 2001], 29–47). For further data on nuclear theft and other opportunities for nuclear terrorism, see Robin M. Frost, *Nuclear Terrorism After 9/11*, Adelphi Paper 378 (London and New York: Routledge, 2005).

5. Matthew Bunn and Anthony Wier, who have been tracking this problem at Harvard University's Managing the Atom Project, wrote in 2004 that 130 research reactors were still operating on HEU, and many with inadequate security (*Washington Post*, September 11, 2004). Since then this number has been reduced—slightly.

6. Allan Lengel, *Washington Post* staff writer (*Washington Post*, September 16, 2005).

7. Pakistan's President Pervez Musharraf confirmed in 2005 that D. A. Q. Khan provided North Korea with centrifuge machines for making enriched uranium that can be used to build nuclear bombs (*New York Times*, August 25, 2005).

8. Walter Laqueur, *The Age of Terrorism*, ch. 2 ("The Philosophy of the Bomb"), esp. 49, 56–57. On nineteenth-century anarchism and its religious precursors, see also James Joll, *The Anarchists* (Cambridge: Harvard University Press, 1980).

9. Haruki Murakami, *Underground* (New York: Vintage, 2000), 361–62 and 301–302. In the assessment by David E. Kaplan and Andrew Marshall, Asahara's goal was "a delusion of fantastic proportions" (*The Cult at the End of the World* [New York: Crown, 1996], 156).

10. The *Stimmung* versus *Haltung* distinction was used by the Nazi authorities in their surveys assessing the reaction of the German

population to the Allied bombing attacks (*The United States Strategic Bombing Survey, European War,* report 64b, "The Effects of Strategic Bombing on German Morale," vol. 1:42–43).

In an analysis of World War II bombing that I conducted shortly after the war, I found further evidence of the "threshold" at which a society's deportment suddenly deteriorates. The elasticity of resources is one key factor. Fred Charles Iklé, *The Social Impact of Bomb Destruction* (Norman: University of Oklahoma Press, 1958).

11. Richard K. Betts, "Fixing Intelligence," *Foreign Affairs* (January-February 2002): 56.

12. Walter Laqueur, *The Age of Terrorism,* 141. In his follow-on study, Walter Laqueur wrote: "Terrorism has been with us for centuries, and it has always attracted inordinate attention. . . . It has been a tragedy for the victims, but seen in historical perspective it seldom has been more than a nuisance." And as to assassinations, Laqueur concluded that "the number of prime ministers and heads of state murdered since the end of the Second World War is in excess of sixty, but it is difficult to think of a single case in which the policy of a country has been radically changed as the result of a terrorist campaign." Laqueur, *The New Terrorism: Fanaticism and the Arms of Mass Destruction* (New York: Oxford University Press, 1999), 3 and 46.

13. Kerensky, quoted in Richard Pipes, *The Russian Revolution* (New York: Knopf, 1990), 336–37.

14. Trotsky, quoted in Philip Selznick, *The Organizational Weapon: A Study of Bolshevik Strategy and Tactics* (Glencoe, Ill.: Free Press, 1966), 254 and 257–63. Selznick's book, although dating from the Cold War, is worth reading today. It offers a sophisticated analysis of the organizational stratagems that a ruthless and cunning dictator can use.

15. Richard Pipes, *The Russian Revolution,* 360–61, 381.

16. Ibid., 407–409.

17. Lothar Kettenacker, "Sozialpsycholgische Aspekte der Führer-Herrschaft," in Gerhard Hirschfeld, ed., *The Führer State* (Stuttgart: Klett-Cotta, 1981), 102 and *passim.* This collection of essays offers a sophisticated reinterpretation of Hitler's political appeal. See also Seymour Martin Lipset, *Political Man: The Social Bases of Politics* (Baltimore: John Hopkins University Press, 1981), 151 and *passim.* For a recent psychological interpretation of political leaders, see Jerrold M. Post, *Leaders and Their Followers in a Dangerous World: The Psychology of Political Behavior* (Ithaca: Cornell University Press, 2004).

18. Jonathan Stevenson, *"We Wrecked the Place": Contemplating an End to the Northern Irish Troubles* (New York: Free Press, 1996), 127.

19. On these Russian extremists, see Simon Saradzhyan and Nabi Abdullaev, "Disrupting Escalation of Terror in Russia to Prevent Catastrophic Attacks," BCSIA Discussion Paper 2005-10, Kennedy School of Government, Harvard University, 2005. Simon Saradzhyan (a foreign policy analyst who worked in Moscow) reports that in 2005 the director of Russia's Federal Security Service (FSB) told his counterparts from the other former Soviet republics the terrorists seek to obtain weapons of mass destruction (7–8).

20. In 1930, Sinclair Lewis was the first American to receive the Nobel Prize for literature, and he received many other honors. But *It Can't Happen Here* was one of Lewis's less highly acclaimed books. In 2004, Philip Roth published the novel *The Plot Against America*, a counterfactual history in which Charles Lindbergh defeats FDR in the 1940 election—a plot even less credible than the earlier and more timely plot used by Sinclair Lewis

21. Arthur M. Schlesinger Jr., *The Disuniting of America: Reflections on a Multicultural Society* (Knoxville, Tenn.: Whittle Direct Books, 1991).

22. A series of scholarly studies have arrived at divergent conclusions. For instance, Walter Hofer et al., *Der Reichstagsbrand: Eine wissenschaftliche Dokumentation* (Berlin, 1972) conclude that the Nazis were culpable for organizing the arson. But other historians argued this conclusion was based on forged documents and that only one person, the Communist-affiliated arsonist Van der Lubbe, was responsible (Eckhard Jesse, "Der Reichstagsbrand—55 Jahre danach," *Geschichte in Wissenschaft und Unterricht* [1988]: 194–219).

23. Oppenheimer's interest in Sr-90 is reported by Jonathan Schell, who cites Joseph Rotblatt as his source in *The Gift of Time: The Case for Abolishing Nuclear Weapons Now* (New York: Henry Holt, 1998), 55.

    On the U.S. nuclear targeting plan for 1962 briefed to President Kennedy, see Scott D. Sagan, *Moving Targets: Nuclear Strategy and National Security* (Princeton: Princeton University Press, 1989), 25.

5. Time to Get Serious

1. A sophisticated and comprehensive report on the projects that are part of the "revolution in military affairs" is Michael G. Vickers and Robert C. Martinage, *The Revolution in War* (Washington D.C.: Center for Strategic and Budgetary Assessment, 2004).

Andrew Marshall (Director of Net Assessment in the U.S. Defense Department) played the leading role in developing this revolutionary perspective as an area of study and to guide the relevant Defense Department decisions.

2. Lowell Wood's *unclassified* contributions on this issue are largely in the form of briefings. A recent example dealing with the gamma-ray color camera is "Finding Nukes . . . at High Speeds and Long Ranges," a briefing given to the Defense Science Board on May 23, 2004. Sadly, Wood's proposals and those of his colleagues at the Lawrence Livermore and Los Alamos National Laboratories did not receive the necessary long-term funding and institutional support for team work to develop and test these important approaches, build prototypes, and find cost-saving improvements.

3. The inadequacy of today's sensors is no secret. False-alarm rates are so high that an effective line of defense could not be established without an economically intolerable blockage of commercial traffic. Other applications of these inadequate sensors are farcical: In December 2005 the FBI and the Energy Department admitted that thousands of searches for radioactive materials had been conducted since 9/11, to look around the country for radioactive devices ("dirty bombs") in parking lots and other easily accessible areas. Unless someone had sprinkled plutonium or cesium in the sidewalk, it seems doubtful this operation would have detected a "dirty bomb" that was reasonably hidden. And a shielded HEU-bomb could not have been detected even if it was in a car parked in the street. But this FBI search did stir up strong complaints from American Muslim organizations, since it was reported that many mosques and homes of Muslims were monitored—from the outside (Mathew L. Wald, "Widespread Radioactivity Monitoring Is Confirmed," *New York Times*, December 24, 2005, A11).

One domestic source of bomb material is the continued use of research reactors that still operate on HEU (see chapter 4, note 5). The last section of chapter 3 deals with the prospect of a new domestic source—the MOX economy. To prevent theft or illicit sales of nuclear materials "at the source" requires greatly improved security for many disparate sources, and not only for the Soviet nuclear detritus, even though Russia now owns by far the largest collection of fissionable material and weapons that need better protection.

4. John Lehman, "Getting Spy Reform Wrong," *Washington Post*, November 16, 2005; Newt Gingrich, "Getting the Lessons of Iraq Exactly Right," *Chicago Tribune*, February 18, 2005.

The case for giving more weight to common sense in the workings of the U.S. government has also been made by Philip K. Howard, *The Death of Common Sense: How Law Is Suffocating America* (New York: Random House, 1994), Paul C. Light, *Thickening Government: Federal Hierarchy and the Diffusion of Accountability* (Washington, D.C.: Brookings Institution Press, 1995), and Jonathan Rauch, *Government's End: Why Washington Stopped Working* (New York: Public Affairs Press, 1999).

5. Stephen Flynn, *America the Vulnerable: How Our Government Is Failing to Protect Us from Terrorism* (New York: HarperCollins, 2004), 50–51. Flynn offers rich and highly disturbing detail about the weak defenses to protect U.S. territory from smuggled weapons at ports and the land border. Flynn also recognizes the limits of going to the "source" and hideouts abroad. "It would seem that we are barely capable of hunting down these violent young men even when they are in our midst" (11).

6. The Quadrennial Defense Review Report of February 6, 2006, mentions the requirement "to locate, tag and track fissile materials rapidly . . . and to deploy specialized teams to render safe nuclear weapons quickly anywhere in the world" (34). And the report adds "the need" for "capabilities to detect fissile materials such as nuclear devices at stand-off ranges" (35). *See* www.defenselink.mil/pubs/pdfs/QDR20060203.pdf.

7. Norman Ornstein, "How Many Warnings Does Congress Need to Protect Itself?" *Roll Call*, May 31, 2005.

8. From 2001 to 2003, the Brookings Institution conducted the Presidential Appointee Initiative (with Paul C. Light as the senior advisor), a study that examined the problem in great detail and made actionable recommendations. Apart from a fine study and a couple of legislative draft proposals in Congress, the initiative ended with zero implementation.

9. Paul Schott Stevens, *U.S. Armed Forces and Homeland Defense: The Legal Framework* (Washington D.C.: CSIS Press, 2001): see section on the Posse Comitatus Act (22–27). The statutory authorities for domestic emergencies include the Insurrection Act, the Stafford Act, and the National Emergency Act of 1974 (ibid., 14–19).

10. Donald M. Nelson, *Arsenal of Democracy: The Story of American War Production* (New York: Harcourt, Brace, 1946), 156, 187, and passim.

11. Colin S. Gray, *Modern Strategy* (Oxford University Press, 1999), 207.

12. Predictably, this extraterritorial repatriation of Haitian refugees was challenged in court in 1993. The lower U.S. court used the UN Proto-

col on refugees to interpret U.S. law, since the relevant U.S. act (the
Refugee Act of 1980) was enacted to conform U.S. law to the UN
Protocol (to which the United States had become party in 1968). But
then the Supreme Court held that neither the UN Protocol nor U.S.
law applies to U.S. actions outside U.S. territory. Alan B. Simmons,
ed., *International Migration, Refugee Flows, and Human Rights in North
America: The Impact of Free Trade and Restructuring* (New York: Center
for Migration Studies, 1995), 283–88.

13. For a purely legal assessment of the UN decision on the Protocol,
see Guy S. Goodwin-Gill, *The Refugee in International Law* (Oxford:
Clarendon Press, 1983), 12–13 and passim.

14. The astounding case in England has been widely reported by British newspapers, e.g., the *Press Association*, the *Birmingham Post*, the
Guardian, and the *Telegraph* all on January 20, 2003, and the *Sun*
on January 19, 2003. The number of Afghan postliberation asylum
applicants in the Netherlands is given by the Dutch report *Migration
and Development Cooperation*, issued by the Advisory Council on International Affairs (The Hague, June 2005), 18.

15. Winston S. Churchill, *Their Finest Hour* (Boston: Houghton Mifflin,
1948), 10 and 357.

16. David Reynolds, *In Command of History: Churchill Fighting and Writing the Second World War* (London: Penguin Books, 2005), 182.

6. Restoration

1. Wesley T. Wooley, *Alternaives to Anarchy: American Supranationalism
Since World War II* (Bloomington: Indiana University Press, 1988).

2. Hedley Bull is quoted here from his magisterial and widely acclaimed
book *The Anarchical Society* (New York: Columbia University Press,
2002 [1st ed., 1977]), 280 and 299. Hedley Bull was professor at the
Australian University, the London School of Economics, and then at
the University of Oxford until his untimely death in 1985.

3. William Nordhaus and James Tobin, "Is Growth Obsolete?," in
National Bureau of Economic Research, *Economic Growth, Fiftieth
Anniversary Colloquium V* (New York: distributed by Columbia University Press, 1972), 1. An excellent assessment of the economist's
changing views of perpetual growth is H. W. Arndt, *The Rise and
Fall of Economic Growth: A Study in Contemporary Thought* (Chicago: University of Chicago Press, 1978). Arndt notes that T. W.
Hutchinson's comprehensive *Review of Economic Doctrines, 1870–
1929* (Oxford: Clarendon Press, 1953) lists not "a single reference,

explicit or implicit, to economic growth as an objective of economic policy."

4. Herman E. Daly is now Professor at the School of Public Policy at the University of Maryland. Among his writings on this topic are *Steady-State Economics* (San Francisco: W. H Freeman, 1977; 2d ed., 1991), and *Beyond Growth: The Economics of Sustainable Development* (Boston: Beacon Press, 1996).

ACKNOWLEDGMENTS

HOW SHOULD AN AUTHOR EXPRESS HIS GRATITUDE to those who unstintingly offered wise counsel, inspiration, and guidance, and who helped disentangle a whirligig of ideas? Perhaps simply by saying "thank you."

Daniel Seligman and I became friends in the 1970s when he worked for *Fortune* magazine. In 1987, Dan joined a Defense Department commission on long-term national strategy, which Albert Wohlstetter and I cochaired. Wohlstetter and I came to esteem Dan highly for his deep understanding of the political and social environment and his ability to bring clarity to the most opaque issues. Dan, you encouraged me to navigate my story to its destined ending without shying painful, yet inescapable conclusions. Thank you for your help and companionship on this journey.

Owen Harries and I celebrated the fall of the Berlin Wall in Sidney, Australia, awed by the end of the Cold War unfolding before our eyes. Four years later, we took advantage of that historic transition as we worked on a project that brought senior U.S. and Russian defense officials together to overcome the strategic thinking of the Cold War. At that time, Owen was editor of *The National Interest*, and he published several articles of mine which provided the foundation for this book. Owen, thank you for inspiring the ambitious agenda of my book and for greatly enriching its themes.

Gerald Aronson (M.D., psychiatrist, and expert on neurology) opened a window for me into the vast realm of brain science. He thus helped me venture a bold forecast about superhuman intelligence systems that nations might learn how to build. Gerry and I have collaborated before. In the 1950s, we worked on a successful RAND project (chapter 3 tells that story). Of course, the proof that superhuman intelligence can be developed is not yet in hand. But thank you, Gerry, for helping me to articulate this portentous vision.

I owe thanks to many others.

Joshua Lederberg, Professor Emeritus at Rockefeller University, had the patience and kindness to advise me on problems of prolonging human lives and on possibilities for brain-computer systems that might reach superhuman intelligence. To my knowledge, Joshua Lederberg is the only Nobel Laureate who actually read my very first book (*The Social Impact of Bomb Destruction*) and even thought well of it.

I am grateful to Paul Kozemchak, Philip Merrill, Wolfgang Schürer, Henry Sokolski, and Lowell Wood for their helpful comments on the finished draft, or on parts of it, and for the guidance and essential data they provided. To Conrad Heede I owe thanks for his always reliable and timely research assistance; and I also want to thank those who preceded Conrad during my long dalliance with this book: Dove Waxman, Steven A. Cook, and Lisette Andreae (for research on German sources). My warmest thanks to Carol Purdey and Terri Silver for their splendid assistance in keeping abreast of ever-changing drafts, reshuffled chapters, and endless endnotes.

CSIS, the Center for Strategic and International Studies in Washington, D.C, offered a wonderfully stimulating home for my project. I am greatly indebted to former CSIS president David M. Abshire for inviting me to join CSIS, and to the current president of CSIS, John J. Hamre, for his gratifying endorsement of my work and for having been so patient as my book kept creeping along. Thank you Dave and John.

At the terminus of the journey, to my delight, a new group of helpful supporters stepped forward—the highly professional team of Columbia University Press, my publisher. From the outset, Senior Executive Editor Peter Dimock was interested in the message of my manuscript and has cheerfully led me by the hand through every turnstile of the publication process. My profound thanks to you, Peter. And thanks to all the other superbly professional staff members of Columbia University Press.

As Samuel Johnson noted, "what is written without effort is in general read without pleasure." If you read this book without pleasure, dear reader, it is not that it was written without effort. Blame the grim message—not the messenger.

INDEX

Irish Republican Army (IRA), 64, 73–74
Islam, ix, xii, 13–14, 23, 112n2
Islamic movements, 15
Islamic societies, 75
Islamists, militant, vii, 59, 60–62, 68–69, 84–85, 89–90
It Can't Happen Here (Lewis), 77, 126n20

Japan, 6–7, 10, 68, 98, 99; nuclear weapons and, 40–44, 55; sarin attacks in, 64, 66–67, 78–80
Jensen, Arthur R., 114n11
Jervis, Robert, 43–44
Jews, 16
Jihadists, vii, 59, 90
John Paul II, Pope, 8, 15, 21–22, 112n1
Johnson, Lyndon B., 119n8
Jordan, 81
Judaism, 112n2

Keats, John, 4
Kennedy, John F., 79
Kerensky, Aleksandr, 70
Khan, Abdul Qadeer, 55, 64, 124n7
Khobar Towers attack, 61
Kim Il Sung, 44
Kissinger, Henry, 119n8
Kurzweil, Ray, 29, 115n12

Lahn, Bruce T., 114n11
language, 29, 116n14
Laos, 55
Laqueur, Walter, 65, 69, 123n2, 125n12
Lawrence Livermore Laboratory, 87, 127n2
Lebanon, 61
Lederberg, Joshua, 114n11

Lehman, John, 127n4
LeMay, Curtis, 47
Lenin, Vladimir, ix, 69–72, 76–77
The Lesser Evil: Political Ethics in the Age of Terror (Ignatieff), 93
Lewis, Sinclair, 77, 126n20
Libya, 55, 64
life extension/prolongation of, 22
Light, Paul C., 128n8
"limits of physics," 89
Lindbergh, Charles, 126n20
London bombings, 81
Los Alamos National Laboratory, 87, 127n2
Lugar, Richard, 54, 86, 122n17

Macauley, Thomas B., 17
Machiavelli, Niccolò, 74
MAD. *See* Mutual Assured Destruction
Madansky, Albert, 119n7
Madrid train bombings, 81
Malenkov, Georgii, 52–53
Manhattan Project, 31–32, 79, 87
Mantoux, Paul, 110n2
Mao Ze-dong, 24
Marlowe, Christopher, 109
Marx, Karl, 15–16, 24, 66
Marxism, xii, 15
McKinley, William, 65
Mein Kampf (Hitler), 72
Melilla asylum seekers, 96
memory, 24, 107, 114n10, 115n13
Mexico, 96
Michelangelo, 20
Middle Ages, 7
Middle East, 3
military: affairs, revolution in, 83–84; history lessons, 82; technology and, 5, 83–84

Mill, John Stuart, 8, 105–106
Milosevic, Slobodan, 70
Mokyr, Joel, 110n2
Morocco, 96
mortality: human, 112n2; rates, 20, 23, 112n2
MOX, 56, 127n3
multiculturalism, 77
Munro, Donald J., 7, 110n2
Murakami, Haruki, 66
Musharrraf, Pervez, 124n7
Muslims, 13–14, 16, 60, 67, 76, 127n3
Mutual Assured Destruction (MAD), 46, 51, 119n8, 120n9

Nagasaki, 40–41
Nanos, Dr. G. Peter, 89
Napoleon III, 11
National Coalition Government, 98–99
National Emergency Act (1974), 128n9
nationalism, 111n7
nations, 10, 111n7
nation-states, 2–4, 10, 105, 111n7
NATO (North Atlantic Treaty Organization), 50, 121n14
Netherlands, 21, 90, 98, 127n14
neurophysiology, 19
neuroscience, viii–ix; control of human brain in, 25–34, 113n7, 114n11, 115nn12–13, 116nn14–16, 117n17
Newman, Robert D., 63
Nietzsche, Friedrich, 59–60, 69, 122–23
Nixon, Richard M., 35–36, 48, 119n8
Nobel, Alfred, 65
Nonproliferation Treaty, 56

North Atlantic Treaty Organization. *See* NATO
North Korea, 43–45, 55–56, 62, 64, 96, 121n14
Norway, 49, 60
nuclear danger, 52–54, 121n14, 121n16
nuclear reactors, 45, 55–57, 63, 124n5, 127n3
nuclear technology, 102
nuclear war plans, 79
nuclear weapons, vii–viii, 39, 62, 118n1, 124n7; accidents/unauthorized use of, 45–49, 119nn7–8, 120n9, 120n11; detection of, 85, 86–89, 127nn2–3, 128nn5–6; deterrence of, 43–45, 119n6; elimination/reduction of, 102; global economy and, 103–104; Japan and, 40–44, 50; mutual deterrence, 49–53, 120n12, 121n14, 121n16; non-use of, 53–57, 103, 122n17; Soviet Union on, 41–45, 47–55, 118n1, 118n4, 119n6, 119n8, 120n9; U.S. and, 39–56, 119n6, 119n8, 120n9; use of, 40–44, 82–83. *See also* Mutual Assured Destruction
Nunn, Sam, 54, 86, 122n17
Nunn-Lugar program, 54, 86, 122n17

Ode to a Nightingale (Keats), 4
Oedipus Rex (Sophocles), 54, 57
Ogburn, William F., 24, 113n5
old age, 20–21, 23, 113n3
Oppenheimer, J. Robert, 79
Oregon, doctor-assisted suicide in, 21

Ornstein, Norman J., 91
Orthodox Christians, 13–14
Ottoman Empire, 12

Pakistan, 55, 64, 79, 124n7
Palestine, 12
PALs. *See* Permissive Action Links
Pastoral Symphony (Beethoven), 4
Payne, Keith, 119n6
Pearl Harbor attack, 94
Peloponnesian war, 82
Penrose, Roger, 115n13
Perle, Richard, 50–51
Permissive Action Links (PALs),
     119n7
Peterson, Peter G., 113n3
"physical capital," 106
Pillsbury, Michael, 32, 117n17
plutonium, 56–57, 122n17, 127n3
Pol Pot, 70
Pontifical Academy of Science, 8
population, world, 2
Presidential Appointee Initiative,
     128n8
"Preventing and Defending
     Against Clandestine Nuclear
     Attack" (report), 87
Proliferation Security Initiative,
     86
Protestant Reformation, xi, 8
Protestantism, 110n4
Putin, Vladimir, 51

Al Qaeda, 62, 81, 85
Qian, Wen-yuan, 7, 110n2
Quadrennial Defense Review, 89,
     128n6

Radical Evolution (Garreau), 115n12
Raffarin, Jean-Pierre, 113n3

railroads, 10–12, 111n7, 112nn8–9
RAND Corporation, 45–47, 49
Reagan, Ronald, 39, 48, 50–52,
     120n12
Refugee Act (1980), 128n12
refugees, 95–98, 128n12, 129n14
Reichstag Fire, 78, 126n22
religions, xi–xii, 2, 15–17; Asian,
     112n2; mortality beliefs among,
     22, 112n2
Renaissance, 7
retirement: age, 23, 113n3; delayed,
     23–24
Reynolds, David, 99, 121n16,
     129n16
*The Rise and Fall of Economic
     Growth* (Arndt), 129n3
Roman Catholics, 8, 13–14
Roman Empire, 59, 101, 106,
     112n2
Roosevelt, Franklin D., 94, 99,
     105, 126n20
Rotblatt, Joseph, 79
Roth, Philip, 126n20
Rumsfeld, Donald, 61–62, 89
Russell, Bertrand, 19
Russia, 7, 10, 13; cults in, 75; Czar-
     ist, 24, 69–72; Federal Security
     Service, 126n19. *See also* Soviet
     Union
Russian Social Democratic Labor
     Party, 71

al-Sadr, Muqtada, x, 75
Saradzhyan, Simon, 126n19
sarin, 64, 66–67, 78–80
Saudi Arabia, 61
Schlesinger, Arthur M., Jr., 77
science: ethics and, 14; life science,
     19–20; technology and, xii–xiii,

science (*continued*)
1–9, 12, 104, 109*n*1, 110*nn*2–4, 111*nn*5–6. *See also* computers; *specific fields*
Semtex explosives, 64
Seneca, 20
Shelley, Mary, 4–5
Shiavo, Terri, 21–22
Sinn Fein, 73–74
Snow, C. P., 111*n*6
Soddy, Fredrick, 118*n*1
Sokolski, Henry, 54–55, 122*n*19
Sophocles, 54, 57
The Sorcerer's Apprentice (Goethe), 4
South Korea, 43–45, 121*n*14
Soviet Union, 36; on nuclear weapons, 41–45, 47–55, 118*n*1, 118*n*4, 119*n*6, 119*nn*8–9, 120*n*9; on "Soviet man," 26, 114*n*8. *See also* Russia
Spain, 73, 96
Sparkman, John, 97
Spencer, Herbert, 16
Spengler, Oswald, 111*n*4
Stafford Act, 128*n*9
Stalin, Joseph V., 24, 44, 121*n*16
"stationary state," 106
Stevens, Paul Schott, 92, 128*n*9
Stock, Gregory, 116*n*16
Strategic Defense Initiative (1983), 51
Strauss, Lewis, 55
Strontium 90, 79
Sudan, 96
Suharto, Raden, 14
suicide, doctor-assisted, 21
superhuman intelligence, ix, 19–20, 104–105; China on, 31–32, 117*n*17; U.S. on, 31–34, 117*n*17

Suppy, Priorities, and Allocation Board, 94
Syria, 12

Taiwan, 12
Tajikistan, 75
Taliban regime, 13, 61, 97–98, 127*n*14
Taylor, Theodore B., 62–63, 85, 124*n*4
technology, vii, 11; China and science, 6–7, 31–32, 110*n*2; detection, 86–89, 127*nn*2–3, 128*n*5; dual use of, xi–xii, 19–20, 36, 54–57, 65, 83; military and, 5, 83–84; nuclear, 102; science and, xii–xiii, 1–9, 12, 104, 109*n*1, 110*nn*2–4, 111*nn*5–6
Tegnelia, Dr. James A., 89
telegraph, 11, 112*nn*8–9
telephones, 11
Teller, Edward, 42
Temple Mount, 16
territorial sovereignty, 94–98
terrorism, ix, 81, 125*n*12; biological, 35, 117*n*18; definitions of, 123*n*2; jihadist/millitant Islamists, vii, 59, 60–62, 68–69, 84–85, 89–90; sabotage *vs.*, 60–61; victims of, 61, 123*n*2. *See also* nuclear weapons; *specific groups*
Thayer, Bradley A., 63
Thucydides, 82
Toynbee, Arnold, 8
travel, long-distance, 11
Trotsky, Leon, 70–71. *See also* dual-power stratagem
Truman, Harry S., 39, 41–42, 99
Turkmenistan, 75

Turney, Jon, 5, 109n1

"two souls," world of, 4–9, 109n1, 110nn2–4, 111nn5–6

"tyranny of distance," 10–11, 112n8

Ultimate Emergency Plan: factors of, 84–86; measures, 86–99, 127nn2–3, 128nn5–6, 128nn8–9, 128n12, 129n14

Unamuno, Miguel de, 59

United Nations (UN), ix, xiii, 94, 99, 102–103; on arms control, 36–37, 41–42, 55, 101, 118n3; Asylum Convention, 95–98, 128n12; Protocol to Asylum Convention, 96–97, 128n12

United States (U.S.), ix, 3, 8, 10, 11, 68, 112n9; attacks on, 44, 60–61, 68, 79–80, 93, 97, 123n2; child labor laws, 23–24; continuity of, 89–92; Declaration of War, 73, 92; defense of, 83–99; democracy and, xiii, 15; mobilization laws of, 92–94, 128n9; nuclear weapons and, 39–56, 119n6, 119n8, 120n9; presidency of, 91–92, 128n8; retirement age in, 113n3; on superhuman intelligence, 31–34, 117n17; territorial sovereignty of, 94–98, 128n12; "two souls" of, 5–6; war plans of, 79

United World Federalists, 102

uranium, 56, 63, 124n7, 127n3

Urex-Plus fuel, 56

U.S. Air Force, 46–47

U.S. Arms Control and Disarmament Agency, 48

U.S. Atomic Energy Committee, 52

U.S. Capitol, 90

U.S. Coast Guard, 96

U.S. Congress, 21, 63–64, 90–94

U.S. Constitution, 5, 106

U.S. Department of Defense, 88

U.S. Department of Energy, 88, 127n3

U.S. House of Representatives, 91

U.S. Marines, 61

U.S. Pentagon, 46–48, 119n7; Defense Science Board, 86–87, 127n2; Defense Threat Reduction Agency, 89

U.S. Senate, 35–36, 97, 119n8

U.S. Strategic Air Command, 47

USS Cole, 61

Uzbekistan, 75

Vandenberg, Arthur, 99

Veblen, Thorstein, 24

Vietnam, reactors in, 45, 55

Vietnam War, 45, 119n8

Viner, Jacob, 44

Voltaire, 20

Wagner, Richard, 87

war plans, 79. See also Ultimate Emergency Plan

We (Zamyatin), 114n8

weapons of mass destruction, ix, 1, 85, 105, 126n19

Weimar Republic, 72, 80

Weinberger, Casper, 48, 50

West Berlin, 119n6

West Virginia, 90

Western Europe, xi, 7–8, 110nn2–4

"Western" intellectuals, 111n6

"Western" society, 110n4

Whitehead, Alfred North, 44, 50, 118n5

Wilson, Woodrow, 99